Alasdair Paine has done us a service by writing this clear, warm, straightforward book about pastoral ministry. Working carefully from Scripture and illustrated by his own (Anglican) experience and that of others in various church contexts, he has given us an accessible and useful resource, especially for young men who might be encouraged towards the work of a pastor.

Christopher Ash
Writer in Residence, Tyndale House, Cambridge

Here from a seasoned minister is a gracious and timely invitation to take up the task of Gospel ministry when desire and opportunity coincide.

Alistair Begg
Founder, Truth for Life

The task of full time ministry is a noble one, but also a daunting one for many considering entering it. Alasdair's book is a brilliant summary of what is involved when anyone wrestles with this challenge. It is brief, biblical, balanced and readable. I warmly recommend it to young, and not so young, Christian men in particular.

Kenny Boyd
Minister, Govanhill Free Church, Glasgow

Those who read Alasdair Paine's regular posts through the St Andrew the Great website, will not be surprised by the biblical, clear, insightful and authoritative tone of this little book. The world is becoming more chaotic and clueless. I pray that God will use this book to raise up an increasing number of people who will flood our Christian training colleges and be equipped to take God's solution into His world. This is both a noble task and one which is desperately nee

Founder, Expos

I had the privilege of receiving Alasdair's guidance and mentorship in my earliest days of ministry. Reading *A Noble Task* reminded me of how special that privilege was. Alasdair's gracious and godly voice echoes through these pages and points readers to the only true source of wisdom for ministry – God's own word. This brief but valuable book speaks much sense and gives rich food for thought and prayer. If you are thinking of vocational ministry, read it and take the advice Alasdair gives. If you are a pastor with the opportunity to mentor and guide young men, keep a stack in your study. I plan to do so, and to hand them out liberally.

Jonathan Griffiths
Lead Pastor, The Metropolitan Bible Church, Ottawa;
Chancellor, Heritage College & Seminary, Cambridge, Ontario

This easily-read book provides an excellent overview of pastoral ministry. Here we get warm, biblical, nuanced, wise, challenging, engaging and inspiring counsel from an experienced and thoughtful pastor. We are also supplied with real life stories to ground it all in lived experience. This will be an essential resource for churches, church leaders and those considering gospel ministry

Andy Mason
Minister, St John's Church, Chelsea;
Mission Director, Co-Mission Network

The future of the church depends upon every generation raising up suitably gifted and qualified pastors. This short and succinct book gives a compelling portrait of the work of a pastor. It is packed with faithful biblical teaching, helpful practical advice, moving personal testimony, pertinent wisdom from the past, and honest advice from current pastors serving in different evangelical churches. It will help anyone who is prayerfully considering if they should serve the Lord in this way, and will encourage everyone to see that being a pastor is both a noble and a necessary task. I pray that the Lord will use this book to help the church identify, train, support, encourage and value the pastors of tomorrow.

John Stevens
National Director, Fellowship of Independent
Evangelical Churches

This outstanding and timely book is exactly what is needed for those considering paid full time Christian work. It is solidly grounded in Biblical teaching and thoroughly practical. I can already think of many to whom I shall recommend it – and anticipate adding numerous others to that list.

William Taylor
Rector, St Helen's Bishopsgate, London

A NOBLE TASK

WHY PASTORING A CHURCH
IS A GREAT ROLE,
AND HOW TO KNOW
WHETHER IT MAY BE FOR YOU

ALASDAIR PAINE

Unless otherwise marked, Scripture quotations are taken from the Holy Bible, New International Version Anglicised Copyright © 1979, 1984, 2011 Biblica. Used by permission of Hodder & Stoughton Ltd, an Hachette UK company. All rights reserved. 'NIV' is a registered trademark of Biblica UK trademark number 1448790

Scripture quotations marked ESV are from *The Holy Bible, English Standard Version*, copyright © 2001 by Crossway Bibles, a publishing ministry of Good News Publishers. Used by permission. All rights reserved. ESV Text Edition: 2011.

Alasdair Paine is the Vicar of St Andrew the Great in Cambridge, UK. Before that, he served churches in Exeter and Bournemouth. He is the author of *The First Chapters of Everything: how Genesis 1-4 explains our world*.

Copyright © Alasdair Paine 2025

print ISBN 978-1-5271-1315-2

ebook ISBN 978-1-5271-1373-2

10 9 8 7 6 5 4 3 2 1

Published in 2025

by

Christian Focus Publications Ltd.,

Geanies House, Fearn, Ross-shire

IV20 1TW, Great Britain.

www.christianfocus.com

Cover design by Daniel van Straaten

Printed and bound by
Bell and Bain, Glasgow

All rights reserved. No part of this publication may be reproduced, stored in a retrieval system, or transmitted, in any form, by any means, electronic, mechanical, photocopying, recording or otherwise without the prior permission of the publisher or a licence permitting restricted copying. In the U.K. such licences are issued by the Copyright Licensing Agency, 4 Battlebridge Lane, London, SE1 2HX www.cla.co.uk

*Here is a trustworthy saying: whoever aspires
to be an overseer desires a noble task.*

1 Timothy 3:1

Contents

1	A Noble Task	1
2	The Nature of the Work	11
3	Qualifications for Office	19
4	The Call?	31
5	Training	43
6	Questions	51
7	True Stories	61
8	Peter's Call	81
	For Further Reading	85

CHAPTER 1

A Noble Task

Here is a trustworthy saying: whoever aspires to be an overseer desires a noble task.

—1 Timothy 3:1

In December 1926, a twenty-seven-year-old doctor, Martyn Lloyd-Jones, left a London medical career in which he was making stellar progress to become pastor of a small church in a steelmaking town in South Wales. His move provoked public astonishment, even reaching the papers. Headlines included this: "Leading Doctor Turns Pastor: Large Income Given Up for £300 a year."

One result of his move was that he was sometimes asked to give his testimony about the sacrifice he'd made. He always refused. On one such occasion, he said, "I gave up nothing. I received everything. I count it the highest honour that God can confer on any man to call him to be a herald of the gospel."[1] Or, as the Apostle Paul put it, the work of the overseer is indeed *a noble task*.

---

1   Iain H Murray, *D. Martyn Lloyd-Jones: The First Forty Years 1899-1939* (Banner of Truth, 1982), p. 121, 150. In two volumes,

This little book is for those considering a similar move (or whose friends might be encouraging them to think about it) from whatever you are presently doing in order to train to be a pastor of a church. For you, too, this might involve a measure of sacrifice because you are likely, if you have the requisite gifts for pastoral ministry, already to be good at what you do. So my plan is to show why the job is so worthwhile, what it involves, the qualifications for office and how you can assess whether God is calling you to it. I have also tried to answer some common questions and included the stories of some long-serving pastors, so you can hear from others what it's been like in their experience.

Because this is specifically about being a pastor of a church, I am addressing men. I want to say at the outset that this is for reasons of Bible, not bigotry: I believe that this is the biblical pattern.[2] I do so while also being absolutely clear that *the ministry of women in Bible teaching is not just to be valued, but to be prized.* In our staff team in Cambridge, I work alongside six women colleagues on our pastoral staff, and we want to continue to point gifted women to appropriate Bible-teaching ministries. But that must be the subject of another book.

It's thirty years since I left my regular job to train for pastoral ministry. In that time, I've had the privilege of serving in three churches: as an assistant in one and as senior minister in two. During this time I've learnt much

---

Murray tells the remarkable story of one of the twentieth century's most influential preachers.

2 For more on this, see, for instance, Claire Smith's *God's Good Design* (Sydney: Matthias Media, 2012) or Carrie Sandom's *Different by Design* (Christian Focus, 2012).

about what the job involves, and have opened my Bible many times to reflect on God's patterns for ministry.

I've also had the privilege of advising many gifted men on the same trajectory. But I've lacked a book to give them to help them along the way. Maybe there's one I've missed. But since I haven't yet discovered it, here goes.

The nobility of the task

I want to start by persuading you that this job is indeed, as Paul puts it to Timothy, *a noble task*. Paul is writing about *oversight*, translating the Greek *episcope* (closely related to the word *episcopos*, an overseer). These are the derivation of the English word 'episcopal' but he's almost certainly not talking about being a bishop as we understand it; rather, this is about the work of leadership and teaching in a local church. However our church leadership is structured, the work of the pastor maps fairly neatly onto this. And Paul tells us that this is a *noble* task. The word translated *noble* is a wider word meaning *good*, but our translators have grasped his point: this is a great job, a worthwhile job, an honourable job – and, as Paul says here, one to aspire to.

It's interesting to consider why Paul feels the need to say this. He's writing to Timothy individually, as an Apostle to a minister of the gospel (and his delegate) in Ephesus. But – as is well-known – Paul's use of the plural *you* in the last verse of the letter hints that he's writing to be overheard, likely by Timothy's congregation. We cannot tell what factors in Ephesus meant that Paul felt the need to stress the nobility of the pastoral office: the list of "not this, not that" in the list of character attributes that follows suggests that maybe people had seen poor examples, and this had made them devalue this role. But whatever the reasons, we still need both individually and corporately (as churches and individuals) to hear the Apostle's words, for we live in a world in which we have experienced bad models of ministry in some places, and in which this role is sometimes regarded by wider society as held only by the wet, the weird and the wicked.

So, Bible in hand, can I persuade you why this task is a noble one?

2 Corinthians: Ambassadors of Christ

First and foremost, we have the privilege of devoting our lives to making known the best, greatest, most momentous news in the world. We have the glorious news of reconciliation with God through our Lord Jesus Christ; we have the surprising news of God's grace; we have the life-saving message of redemption; we have a ministry which is eternal and unfading in its consequences. 'Therefore, we are ambassadors for Christ, God making his appeal through us' (2 Cor. 5:20, ESV).

All this is what Paul says of his own ministry in 2 Corinthians, but derivatively, it's also true of any who preach the Apostolic message. Of course, anyone who speaks for Christ is His ambassador – you don't need to be a pastor to do that – but imagine being set apart to give all our working time for this! Could there be a greater project, or a more wonderful Lord to devote our gifts to?

Jesus' resurrection encounter with Peter

You'll know the occasion, written up in the last chapter of John's gospel. The Lord met His disciples for a fish breakfast on the shores of Galilee. The first person He wanted to talk to was Peter – the same Peter who'd let Him down so badly on the night before the cross. In a beautiful act of restoration, mirroring Peter's threefold denial, three times the Lord asked Peter whether he loved Him, and each time gave him a similar instruction: 'Feed my lambs … Take care of my sheep … Feed my sheep' (John 21:15-17).

Jesus' concern for His people to be shepherded could not be clearer. If Peter loved Jesus, then he was to care for Jesus' people. And, to be more specific, Peter was to *feed* them. It is very hard not to see an implication of the profound importance of the pastor's specific role of nourishing the flock by teaching them.

The preciousness of the church

There is a strong emphasis on church leadership in Acts. Two well-known examples are the meeting called by the Apostles to allow them to continue focussing on the crucial ministry of Word and prayer while the church grows (Acts 6:1-7) and Paul's famous speech to the elders at Miletus (Acts 20:13-38).

It is in this speech at Miletus that Paul says, 'Keep watch over yourselves and all the flock of which the Holy Spirit has made you overseers. Be shepherds of the church of God, which he bought with his own blood' (Acts 20:28). The church is so precious to God that He paid for it in blood!

Have you ever had to look after something very precious to someone? I remember one time when my neighbour, who worked for a bank, went on holiday and left me two external hard drives to look after which he judged too precious to leave in an empty house. He must have trusted me! I was so glad when he returned and I was able to hand them back to him unscathed.

Again we see, then, that Jesus' people are deeply precious to Him. No wonder He is concerned that they are well looked after. The astounding honour of the pastor is to do this work on the Lord's behalf.

An astonishing Apostolic decision

The book of Acts also gives us a less well-known example which points to the sheer importance of church leadership.

Acts 13–14 tell us the gripping story of Paul and Barnabas' first missionary journey. From their sending church in Syrian Antioch they sailed to Cyprus, and then north to the mainland cities of Perga, Pisidian Antioch, Iconium, Lystra and Derbe. They preached the gospel to great effect, but also endured huge opposition: expulsion from Pisidian Antioch, a plot to stone them in Iconium, and actual stoning in Lystra. They arrived at their final destination, Derbe, with emotional and physical injuries.

Bruised and battered, they now took an astonishing decision. It was time to head back to their sending church in Syrian Antioch. If you look at a map, you'll see that from Derbe it is not that far by direct journey south-east. But instead, they took a far longer route, retracing their steps through the very cities where they'd been beaten and opposed – giving themselves not only weeks longer on the road, but putting themselves back in harm's way. And why? To encourage the new disciples they'd left in each of these towns, and 'to appoint elders for each church' (Acts 14:21-24). Nothing could indicate more clearly how concerned Paul and Barnabas were that these new little churches had leadership than the risks they took to secure it.[3] Churches need pastors!

---

3 Later, Paul reminds Timothy of this dangerous back-and-forth when he writes to Timothy (2 Tim 3:11): one which Timothy saw part of, for he was from Lystra. Once again, Paul's aim is to encourage a Christian leader to stay in post, and to stay firm, and to serve his people.

The *very existence* of the Pastoral Epistles

The fact that three whole letters of the New Testament (1 and 2 Timothy and Titus) are specifically addressed to gospel ministers, and whose subject is gospel ministry, should alert us to the importance of this work in God's eyes. *Churches need pastors*. The Apostle Paul is deeply concerned for the health of the churches in Ephesus and Crete, and it's to these ministers that he writes. Indeed, it's clear throughout that the spiritual health of these churches to a large extent rides on the spiritual health of these men. Their work is to include the vital business of appointing other men as local church leaders. Pastors are at the heart of God's plans for His people.

We need to recover this emphasis. Since, perhaps, the 1960s there has been a right reaction against over-clericalism and a stress on every-member ministry; there has also been a recovery of the Reformation doctrine of the priesthood of all believers and the value of all work as a vocation. Rightly, we've been reminded that we can be Christians in law, in politics, in teaching, in business and so on. We have learnt to refute a spirituality which placed pastors and missionaries on a spiritual pedestal. These have been important corrections, but the danger is that this thinking can make us too settled in these professions – which are normally better paid! The existence of three whole books of the Bible – the pastoral epistles, specifically devoted to the pastoral ministry – helps reset the balance by showing that the minister's work really matters: both in God's eyes, and for the health of the churches.

Colossians: Presenting real people mature in Christ

As Paul wrote to the Colossians about Jesus, 'He is the one we proclaim, admonishing and teaching everyone with all wisdom, so that we may present everyone fully mature in Christ' (Col. 1:28). The work of the minister is to help people to grow to maturity. We have the privilege of seeing people come to know Christ and for Him to transform them. One of the privileges of serving a local church over a period of time is that of seeing Him work in people.

Just recently we were listening to the groom's speech at a wedding. He'd first come to us as an unbeliever; Christ got to work in him and it's been simply wonderful watching him change and grow. His speech was full of the Lord Jesus. What sheer joy and delight there is in having a part to play in this – and as the years go by, you see it more and more. What a noble task indeed!

The Lord Jesus' call to prayer in Matthew 9

Finally, consider Jesus' great call to prayer for workers for the harvest field in Matthew 9. He starts with the same picture, of sheep needing shepherds. Then, switching the illustration from pastoral to arable farming, He gives this famous analysis: 'The harvest is plentiful, but the workers are few. Ask the Lord of the harvest, therefore, to send out workers into his harvest field' (Matt. 9:37-38).

Jesus' analysis is so instructive. Some would have us believe that the apparent decline of Christianity in the UK is because Christianity has been proved wrong or out of date. But have we considered the Lord's view – that a critical need could be lack of gospel workers? Lift your eyes to see the need!

In our church, when a student from elsewhere in the country comes to trust Christ, we try to find a church in their home town which teaches the Bible. Sometimes, despite searching widely, we draw a blank. This may reflect our ignorance, but the startling truth seems to be emerging that there are whole towns across the UK with no reliable Bible-teaching church. No wonder, then, if the public profile of Christianity is declining: our pulpits are not supplied with faithful preachers! No doubt the Lord has a wider category of harvest workers in mind than local church pastors, but they are surely key.

A member of our church who's recently started training for pastoral ministry has his own story of this. He and his parents came to a personal faith in Christ as a direct result of a new pastor being appointed to their village church who began to open the Bible with them. With this wonderful mercy of God fresh in his mind, now he wants to go and do the same!

History also bears out the huge difference local pastors can make to the whole cause of the Lord Jesus. The great revival of the eighteenth century is well-known and rightly associated with the names of the great itinerant evangelists George Whitefield and John Wesley. Less well-known is that a crucial component of the revival was the work of ordinary pastors preaching Christ in their local churches and districts: Romaine, Venn and many others in London; Grimshaw in Haworth in Yorkshire; Fletcher at Madeley in Shropshire; Rowlands in Llangeitho, Wales; Walker in Truro, Cornwall – the list goes on and on.[4] Through their efforts, under God, many thousands were converted: indeed, the whole country was changed.

What would it take to see the gospel spread across the our world again? A great work of the Spirit of God, of course, for which we pray. But both Jesus' own words and history

---

4 If you can find a second-hand copy, G R Balleine's *A History of the Evangelical Party in the Church of England* (2nd ed, 1951) tells the stories of many of these pastors. J C Ryle's *Christian Leaders of the Eighteenth Century* (1885) gives highlights and is easier to get hold of.

indicate that the Lord will answer this prayer by raising up workers for His harvest field.

Am I, then, beginning to persuade you that *whoever aspires to be an overseer desires a noble task*?

CHAPTER 2

The Nature of the Work

"What does Dick *do* all day? Show tourists round the church?"

Our minister at St Helen's, Bishopsgate, London, Dick Lucas, was recalling a question a friend of his mother had asked her in his early years as Rector. It reflects the bafflement many feel about how a pastor fills his time if they only encounter him on the odd Sunday, or at Christmas, a wedding or a funeral. Sunday (or sometimes Saturday) appears to be the only working day: six days invisible, one day incomprehensible!

As you can imagine, rather more is involved. This chapter is about what's in the job description – so that you can picture whether this could be you.

A pastor's exact role varies with church size, denominational arrangements and local expectations. There are likely to be many entries in a pastor's diary: Sunday services, baptisms, weddings and funerals; meetings with colleagues, elders or church council; evangelistic and pastoral visiting; teaching courses; attending ministers' fraternals; one-on-one Bible reading, pastoral counselling, and more. All these are in addition to the time for study, preparation, prayer, writing projects and answering emails! Nevertheless, again with Bibles in our hands, we can identify *one great aim* and *three key activities* which are at the heart of the role, whatever the church.

Our aim: presenting everyone mature in Christ

The Apostle Paul describes his aim as to 'present everyone fully mature in Christ' (Col. 1:28). His teaching, his prayers and his strategy were all devoted to this great objective: that he might present (before Jesus) people who'd come to know Christ and had grown into Christian maturity.

He shows us what maturity looks like on the previous page of his letter: living lives 'worthy of the Lord, pleasing Him in every way, bearing fruit in every good work, growing in the knowledge of God, being strengthened to endure,' and being filled with enthusiastic thankfulness for our deliverance in Christ (Col. 1:10-13). This is Paul's great aim in all his work, and surely – for we serve the same Lord – it must be the purpose of every pastor.

It sounds obvious but let me say it: being a pastor is about *people*. It's about helping them to know Christ and grow in maturity in Him. Our great aim is not maxing sermon downloads, but presenting real people mature in Christ. It is *people* who are the fruits of our ministry, or, as Paul put it elsewhere, our letters of recommendation (2 Cor. 3:1-2).

So then: do you long for people to come to know Christ and be saved for ever? For them to grow in godly assurance, joy, character and usefulness? Would you like to see your life invested in such a way that, on the last day, you may "present" people, with lives transformed, to the Lord Jesus?

Seeing people grow in Christ – what a privilege and joy! In ministry, we have the privilege of seeing the Lord work through our meagre efforts.

But how on earth is this to be achieved?

The ministry of the Word

Our equipment is the Bible. Paul reminds his younger colleague Timothy that 'All Scripture is God-breathed and is useful for teaching, rebuking, correcting and training in righteousness, so that the servant of God may be thoroughly equipped for every good work' (2 Tim. 3:16-17). It seems that Paul is thinking here particularly of the pastor-teacher or gospel worker: the phrase NIV translates *servant of God* is actually *man of God* in the Greek, echoing a term often used in the Old Testament for a prophet.

The place of the Bible in the minister's life and work was a rediscovery of the Reformation. Before then, it was the custom at an English ordination service for the bishop to present the candidates with a chalice – a communion cup – as a symbol of their main work. Now – ever since the Reformation – the bishop presents a Bible instead. The minister is to be a minister of the Word.

In all his work, then, the pastor will be wanting to share, teach and preach the Bible. When he meets the sick or troubled person, he will want to share Scripture with them. Every baptism, wedding or funeral is an opportunity to preach Christ. A healthy minister will be seeking every opportunity his ordinary work affords him to bring the Bible to bear and to help people know God through it – and if there is no such opportunity, to question the usefulness of that activity. He will be wanting to train others to share in this work, so that the church may continue and grow

(2 Tim. 2:2). He will have in his mind that the church will only grow with this nourishment.

Central to this is the ministry of preaching. Certainly, this is how Paul sees it: he follows his comments about the minister's equipment with a charge of great solemnity, 'In the presence of God and of Christ Jesus, who will judge the living and the dead, and in view of his appearing and his kingdom, I give you this charge: preach the word …' (2 Tim. 4:1-2a). It must be front and centre in our work. As Paul also told Timothy, 'Devote yourself [strong word!] to the public reading of Scripture, to preaching and to teaching' (1 Tim. 4:13). A regular ministry of faithful preaching can transform many lives.

I personally try to keep the mornings clear of appointments so that I can study God's Word and books that will help me grasp it, teach it, and to prepare for talks and other teaching opportunities. I do my best to listen to God's surprising Word and try – however imperfectly – to progress at explaining it to real people. This is an irreducible element of the pastor's job, whatever other expectations may be placed on him (and he may need to fight some of them off if he is to achieve it).

So then: do you love God's people and His Word in such a way that you will labour to study, and to prepare accurate, nourishing, easy-to-listen-to, applicable Bible teaching?

Prayer

All Christians have the privilege of prayer, and all are called to pray; but ministers of the gospel are particularly called to pray. Certainly this was the pattern of the Apostles, where they say that they will 'give [their] attention to prayer and the ministry of the word' (Acts 6:4). Likewise, pastors are normally set apart from other work so that they can devote themselves to these things. The Lord Jesus prayed for His disciples; Paul shows us in his letters how he prays for those he's writing to. How can a ministry which is all about presenting people mature in Christ – based as that is on God's work – not include a significant element of prayer?

In practice, the gospel minister will set aside some time – probably additional to his morning devotional quiet time – to pray for those in his care, and those he's seeking to reach for Christ. He will be with his lists.

Over the years, he should have the inestimable joy of seeing the Lord answer his prayers in the lives of individuals, even beyond his wildest prayers and dreams. Sadly, along the way, there will be disappointments – as the Lord taught us to expect in the parable of the sower. But he should also see real growth: seed watered by prayer, grown by the Lord (2 Cor. 3:7).

Do you know the struggle and joy of intercessory prayer? Will you be prepared to give yourself to this?

The direction of the church

'Presenting everyone mature in Christ' requires not just personal and public preaching, but directing the church so that its policies, people and practices promote this. In 1 Timothy 5, Paul gives Timothy instructions about church policies: on widows, on ministerial pay and on handling of allegations against those in leadership, and it's clear Paul expected his younger colleague to take a lead in implementing these.

When you think about it, it's noteworthy that the earthly leadership of churches – both in the New Testament and down the centuries since – is given to pastors, rather than

CEOs or administrators. I take it that this arrangement – assumed in Scripture and followed down in church history – reflects the fact that the Lord Jesus is the head of the church, and He leads by His Word. Therefore, earthly leaders need to be those who are best versed in the Bible, so that every policy seeks to implement scriptural principles, and, more than that, is a teaching opportunity. And, of course, the church is led from the pulpit. But the flip side is that pastors will be involved in leadership and policy decisions.

Paul also gives Timothy and Titus a great deal of instruction about appointments – instructions we'll return to in the next chapter. The space Paul gives to this suggests that for Paul this is a crucial part of the minister's role. A predecessor of mine here in Cambridge used to say that his only spiritual gift was appointing assistant ministers. I think he was being modest, but he hit the nail on the head in understanding this as a key part of his role. I am so thankful for colleagues I have been able to appoint, and what a difference they make to the life of our church!

We must be careful at this point. None of this is saying that the pastor is to be the sole governor of the church – it's clear in the pastoral epistles that leadership has a corporate dimension. Moreover, it is not the case that the pastor needs to, or should, lead on every detail of policy. It is unwise, unbiblical and impracticable for the pastor to attempt this (and this is why the supply of helpers with admin, finance, safeguarding etc is a key need to pray for). You absolutely don't need to be an expert on these things, nor should they be your job.

Rather, the pastor's role in policy must mainly be in his teaching, which creates a culture and a shared understanding of mission within which others will make wise decisions. He must stick, as his priority, to the ministry of the Word of God. Paul talks about pastor-teachers being among those given by God "to equip his people for works of service" (Eph. 4:11-12). I take it that this implies that as the pastor does his main job of teaching, he will be shaping the attitudes and gospel understanding of the treasurer, the safeguarding officers, the administrators, the musicians and others so that they do their jobs with Bible attitudes and priorities. I have found that if I stick to my job, others will be better at doing theirs!

Nevertheless, because the pastor is a leader, he will inevitably be involved in the making of a lot of decisions, and at least some of the paraphernalia that goes with that: meetings, interviews, reading and writing emails, chewing his pencil as he thinks about policies. Sometimes, he will need to make tough decisions and will need courage. Occasionally, he will need to be involved – with others – in the painful but necessary matter of church discipline. He will find himself spreading all these matters before the Lord and pleading often for wisdom.

Inescapably, then, the pastor is a leader. Of course, this must be leadership exercised gently, after the pattern of Christ. He must never be a dictator. But he will still have much responsibility on his shoulders, and he will need to face it and exercise it.

So then, here are three key roles for the pastor. Clearly they are pretty significant. All this leads naturally to the question: who is qualified for this?

CHAPTER 3

Qualifications for Office

Given the high level of responsibility that a pastor bears, it should not surprise us that the New Testament insists on certain qualifications for this office. In this chapter we'll investigate those. Much of this we'll find in the pastoral epistles, where Paul lays out two fascinating lists of requirements for *overseers* (1 Tim. 3) and *elders* (Titus 1) – probably two words for the same thing, and both of which look close to the office of pastor. We'll see the Bible's surprising priorities. But first, we need to cover one essential preliminary.

You must be born again

This, of course, is what the Lord Jesus told Nicodemus, the member of the Jewish ruling council who came to see Him one night (John 3:1-21). The Lord told this senior figure in the religious hierarchy that he needed this radical inward change, brought about by the Holy Spirit, if he was even to see the kingdom of God, let alone enter it.

These words are, of course, for all people, not just for aspirant ministers. You may have heard the story of the woman who asked George Whitefield, "Sir, why are you always preaching on 'You must be born again'?" To which Whitefield replied, "Madam, because you must!" But we can surely not help being struck by the fact that Jesus didn't speak these words to some random pagan, but to a man who nowadays we'd regard as a religious top dog. Even *he* needed to be born again.

It's scarily possible to be in ministry and yet not born again. Years ago, when I was considering ministry, I went to an interview at a theological college. The kindly tutor welcomed me and showed me to my chair. Then, looking me in the eye, he asked his opening question: "How do you know that your sins are forgiven?" It was – and is – quite a question! Later, I learned his story: he'd been in parish ministry in the Church of England for some years without a real, personal knowledge of Christ. The question makes me think he'd been relying on his own goodness in some way. Marvellously, he'd later come to grasp the gospel. But he didn't want others to make the same initial mistake – for such ministers are worse than useless. (I have subsequently used the same question in many ministry recruitment interviews.)

In his remarkable book, *Lectures to my Students*, Victorian preacher Charles Spurgeon starts by emphasising the dangers of being unconverted and in ministry. "A graceless pastor is a blind man elected to a professorship of optics, philosophising upon light and vision, discoursing upon and distinguishing to others the nice shades and delicate blendings of the prismatic colours, while he himself is absolutely in the dark!"[1]

---

1 C H Spurgeon, *Lectures to my Students* (1875), first lecture, "The minister's self-watch."

We need, then, to heed Jesus' many words about hypocrites and blind guides. Do we really know Christ? Are our motives for ministry those of a truly converted person, or are we in it because we like the sound of our own voices, enjoy the limelight and the power, or are we there because we want to tell of a Jesus we've genuinely come to know, because He's got hold of us?

What about my CV or résumé?
The surprising lists in the pastoral epistles
Turning now to Paul's requirements for the overseer or elder in 1 Timothy 3 and Titus 1, we encounter a surprise. Paul's instructions on these appointments don't focus on the criteria we might consider: gifts of personality or learning. Instead, he's interested in how a candidate for ministry conducts himself in his daily life. What's he like at home? What sort of husband and father is he? How does he treat those he interacts with? Are there known defects in his character, such as being a bully, or having a short temper? What's his attitude towards money or drink? What's his reputation with outsiders like? While we might be interested in a man's CV, Paul insists that top priority be given to a man's conduct, and typical patterns of behaviour – things you can't see on a CV.

The reasons for this emphasis are not hard to deduce. Above all else, Paul's concern for the church shines through. Here are the Lord's people, who are deeply precious to God! So before anyone is given a position of significant authority in the church, we need to know that they can be trusted.

Perhaps lying behind the Apostle's "not this … not that …" set of negatives ("not given to drunkenness, not violent but gentle, not quarrelsome, not a lover of money…") he has some horror stories which he's observed of ministry being undermined, and people damaged, by ministers for whom this is a problem. For him, the best way to deal with this is to be careful at the point of selection.

Moreover, Paul teaches that the "knowledge of the truth leads to godliness" (Titus 1:1), and this being so, we'd expect the teacher of the truth to have been moulded towards godliness by that same truth.

Paul is also reflecting the power of example, an important part of the minister's role in the pastoral epistles: "Set an example for the believers in speech, in conduct, in love, in faith, in purity" (1 Tim. 4:12); "In everything set them an example by doing what is good" (Titus 2:7). The minister's life can preach a powerful sermon: people are interested in how leaders live and cannot be blamed for some curiosity about whether they practise what they preach. Conversely, a fly in the ointment of the pastor's conduct can stop people listening to him even more effectively than a microphone failure or a persistently crying baby.

In many ways, the requirements Paul makes are self-explanatory. Some notes:

- "Faithful to his wife" (1 Tim. 3:2, Titus 1:6) is the NIV translation of what could more literally be rendered *a one-woman man*. When a minister becomes involved in an affair, the results impact not just his family but the whole church. The sin of pornography use, even though hidden, will undermine his witness and his ability to help others.

- "Temperate, self-controlled, not violent but gentle, not quarrelsome" (1 Tim. 3:2-3) are primarily about our interactions with people, of which ministry

Qualifications for Office

brings so many. How do you typically respond when people or circumstances are frustrating? Is there anything in you which bullies to get your way?

- "He must manage his own family well and see that his children obey him" (1 Tim. 3:4; see also Titus 1:6). This is because the church is a family. Paul makes the (fairly) obvious observation that a man incapable of leading his own family well is unsuitable for leading a church. I have heard it said that this rules out of pastoral ministry those whose children turn away from the faith in adulthood, but I do not think this is what he has in view, for even the best parents cannot engineer the new birth. Nor can it mean that home life is entirely free of strife – dream on! More likely the Apostle has in mind the father who neglects his family or exercises no authority or discipline – with predictably wild results. If it's like that in his home, what will it be like in the church? (Incidentally, this does not mean the minister must be married, or Paul likely would have had to rule himself out.)

- "Hospitable" (1 Tim. 3:2; Titus 1:8) matters not just because the minister's home is to be a place of welcome and food (itself a very powerful way to minister) but also, at a deeper level, because the minister needs to be a lover of people. I say again: the job is about people! Do you show hospitality? Even if you may struggle with it, do you have a love for people that will want to welcome them?

- "Not given to drunkenness, not a lover of money" (1 Tim. 3:3) and "not pursuing dishonest gain"

(Titus 1:7) remind us that ministers are not exempt from temptations common to us all; sadly, in both these areas, some ministers have gone under.

- "He must not be a recent convert, or he may become conceited and fall under the same judgment as the devil" (1 Tim. 3:6). Generally, caution should be exercised before heading too soon from conversion to ordination. There is so much that God has to teach us, and so many ways we need to be humbled and grow. That does not mean that when we're converted we might not begin to have thoughts of ministry, but there will normally be some years in which we can mature in the faith, and be able to display the patterns of conduct seen in this list.

- "He must also have a good reputation with outsiders, so that he will not fall into disgrace and into the devil's trap" (1 Tim. 3:7). For the credibility of the church and its evangelistic mission, reputation matters. Paul is interested in what non-Christian colleagues and friends think of a candidate for ministry. We churchgoers see the man on Sunday; what's he like in the office on Monday? The "devil's trap" may be to reflect the devil's desire to discredit the church, as a leader is found wanting in some moral area which non-Christians sadly notice. That doesn't mean colleagues have to agree with him in everything, of course. I remember a documentary about a well-known Christian musician. A non-Christian colleague was interviewed. "I don't share his religion", the colleague said, "but you won't find any dirt on him at all."

Qualifications for Office

Help!

You might find that reading this list makes you rule yourself out immediately. It's worth remembering, then, that Paul is not talking about sinless perfection. Ministers are sinners, too. Many times, I've come back in my mind's eye to the Lord Jesus' words to Peter, "Feed my sheep" (John 21:17), coming as they do after Peter's denial of his Lord. I've been so helped to be reminded of the Lord's forgiveness, and that He can still use us in ministry. Looking back, I can think of many times (and many more I must have forgotten) when I have failed. That is the story of all of us.

And yet, at the same time, Paul's requirements stand. In our patterns of conduct, we must be able to keep Paul's positives and avoid his negatives. Sin must not be left unaddressed. James warns us that "Not many of you should be teachers, my fellow believers, because you know that we who teach will be judged more strictly" (James 3:1).

It's because conduct really matters that in our own ministry staff recruitment, we put very heavy weight on references. Secular employers often ask for them as an afterthought, and don't probe the candidate's character. But the implication of what Paul says is that it would be wise to go to the referees at an early stage in the process.

I say again, though: don't be defeated. All of the requirements we've seen so far are ones to which any godly person should aspire – not just a minister. It's just that in the minister they should be writ large. Whoever we are, we need to wage war against sin in our lives and seek the joy of repentance and progress.

Are you, then, able to look through this list of requirements and know that, while not perfect, you meet them? It would be sensible to ask someone who knows you well to review the list with you.

Holding firmly to the trustworthy message

Paul tells Titus that the elder "must hold firmly to the trustworthy message as it has been taught, so that he can encourage others by sound doctrine and refute those who oppose it" (Titus 1:9). Here is a requirement which is less moral and more credal. As false teaching infected the Cretan churches, it is essential that Titus appoint teachers of the truth. They absolutely need to hold to "the trustworthy message as it has been taught" – that is, the Apostolic message – and to hold "firmly" to it.

This doesn't mean that we've never experienced a measure of doubt in some aspect of our faith, or that we have encyclopaedic doctrinal knowledge. But it does mean that we need to be persuaded of the great essential truths of the Bible in such a way that not only do we live by them, but that we fully own them, and want to teach and defend them. Teaching the truth can bring a ton of bricks on our heads: we will only be sustained in doing so over the long run if we are convinced we are telling the truth.

Moreover, ministers who teach error (other than the minor, honest mistakes we all make) are a terrible menace. Paul found on Crete that "they are disrupting whole households by teaching things they ought not to teach" (Titus 1:11).

For this reason, many denominations insist that candidates for ministry sign a doctrinal statement. You will do well to work through one of these thoughtfully, and to read and absorb reliable books of Christian doctrine, which will strengthen your faith, deepen your understanding and answer your questions. A good theological college will also help with this – which is why it's essential to pick one where the college, too, "holds firmly to the trustworthy message as it has been taught." And be encouraged: if we are faithful students of the Bible, we'll find that the Bible itself builds our faith.

Do you hold firmly to the Apostolic message?

Able to teach

Did you see that little phrase almost hiding there in 1 Timothy 3:2, tucked in with all the moral requirements for ministry? The other requirements are all those which we should expect in any mature Christian, but here's one that is specifically for the overseer. He must be "able to teach."

These three English words translate a single Greek one, *didaktikos*, rendered in my Greek lectionary as "skilful in teaching".[2] We've already seen that preaching the Word of God is at the heart of the pastor's role, so obviously he needs to be able to do that. The adjective recurs in 2 Timothy 3:24, where the servant of God, when confronting error, must be "able to teach."

There is surely a big overlap here with holding firmly to Apostolic truth, because no teacher can be described as able to teach if they do not know their subject. He needs to be one, also, who "correctly handles the word of truth" (2 Tim. 2:15), and training in knowing how to handle Bible passages is so important for this. But perhaps Paul also implies a gift as a communicator, for we need to be able to put these truths across to regular people. For all this, the

---

2 Walter Bauer, *A Greek-English Lexicon of the New Testament and Other Early Christian Literature* (hereafter BDAG), rev. and ed. Frederick W. Danker, 3rd ed. (University of Chicago Press, 2000).

preacher needs the qualities of mind – powers of analysis and speech – that a good instructor in any subject will have.

Normally, there's only one way to find out. Seek opportunities to give Bible talks and ask for feedback. And don't judge your results based on very few talks. Keep at it and see if you improve to the point where people genuinely find your talks nourishing. But if this isn't your gifting, there's no shame in recognising that.

Can you teach?

* * *

Looking back over Paul's requirements, I'm struck again by the dignity of the office of elder/pastor/overseer. As Philip Towner memorably puts it in his commentary on the pastoral epistles, "To put the overseer code into proper perspective, the importance and urgency of the church's evangelistic mission require that its leaders be of the highest caliber."[3]

Willing to suffer
We've spent time in 1 Timothy and Titus, but in between them is 2 Timothy – probably Paul's last New Testament letter. Here he's concerned for his younger colleague to keep on ministering in the face of discouragements and opposition. Part of the Apostle's message is that Timothy is to expect suffering and be willing to endure it. "Join with me in suffering, like a good soldier of Christ Jesus" (2 Tim. 2:3). The theme recurs many times in the letter. Gospel ministry is a high privilege, a noble task – but it involves suffering. It did for the Lord Jesus, it did for Paul, and it will for Timothy. When we recruit for staff posts at our church, we list as one of the specifications, "willing to suffer for

---

3 Philip H. Towner, *1-2 Timothy and Titus* (IVP, 1994), p. 89.

the gospel" (2 Tim. 1:8). Not at all because our church is a terrible place to work – far from it – but because suffering of various kinds may come the pastor's way. Pastors can face opposition from some, outside the church and sometimes, sadly – as in 2 Timothy – from within. We may at times find ourselves in situations of loneliness or insecurity. We will bear the heartache of people's own struggles and sometimes be bitterly disappointed. The work can be hard. Paul memorably describes the gospel minister's role as being like that of a soldier, an athlete and a farmer (2 Tim. 2:4-6), all occupations which involve struggle and difficulty.

All this said, this shouldn't be a showstopper. *All* Christians are to take up their cross and follow the Lord Jesus. Moreover, what leadership role is there in life which does not involve struggle and risk? And we must never forget the Lord's promise, given to those on His mission: "And surely I am with you always, to the very end of the age" (Matt. 28:20). Every pastor can tell how, even in the difficulties, the Lord walks with us and provides for us.

All these requirements are necessary conditions for the pastor – but are they sufficient? What about the 'call' to ministry? To this we now turn.

CHAPTER 4

The Call?

In a recent survey of younger adults from Bible-teaching churches, one of the top reasons given for not heading to pastoral ministry was "I don't feel called".

This surely raises some questions. What is meant by "a call" to ministry? What would it feel like? How would we know if God were calling us? In this chapter, we'll seek to nail this vital subject.

At the risk of oversimplification, there are two opposite views. On the one hand, some writers emphasise the absolute necessity of a definite, felt, divine call, without which we must not enter ministry. In his classic *Lectures to my Students*, Charles Spurgeon compares this to the call of the prophets in the Old Testament. Then, in considering the New Testament evidence, he argues that since ambassadors are appointed by the monarch, and since we are ambassadors for Christ (2 Cor. 5:20), pastors must be appointed by God Himself. He points out that, as Paul told the Ephesian elders, it is the Holy Spirit who has made us overseers (Acts 20:28); and that Paul also tells us that it is

God himself who gave pastors and teachers to the church (Eph. 4:11). Thus, Spurgeon reasons, we must obviously and clearly be appointed by God. He dreads men coming into public ministry who are not called. He quotes a writer who said, "Do not enter the ministry if you can help it."[1]

On the other hand, some have said that this idea of a specific call is overblown, and that rather than not entering ministry if we can help it, *all* of us should be asking what our excuse is for *not* doing it.

The obvious danger of the first approach is that men who would be suitable for ministry don't enter it. Perhaps they are waiting for a particular experience they identify with "the call", which never comes. The danger of the second is that unsuitable candidates enter pastoral ministry, with predictably unhappy results.

My own view, which is that of the older Christian denominations, is that it is right and reasonable to think in terms of a "call" to ministry. We are not the prophets of old, but, given the great responsibility that being a pastor involves, it is surely right that we should not think of embarking on this without assurance that God Himself wants *us* to do this work. In *The Book of Common Prayer*, the bishop asks candidates at an ordination, "Do you trust that you are inwardly moved by the Holy Ghost to take upon you this Office and Ministration, to serve God for the promoting of his glory, and the edifying of his people?"[2] Other denominations make similar enquiries at their ordinations. Without such an assurance we'll surely find it harder to stick at the task when the going gets tough, and we will worry that we were being presumptuous.

---

1 Charles Spurgeon, *Lectures to my Students*, chapter 2, "The Call to the Ministry."

2 Book of Common Prayer (1662): service for the ordering of deacons.

However, it is unhelpful to think of this call in the same terms as that experienced by the prophets of the Old Testament. The pastor today is not a writer of God's Word: while the Word of God came to the prophets, today, the pastor comes to the Word! And, notably, the recruitment of ministers in the New Testament does not come as a purely personal call, but involves the church; it needs to be a careful and thorough corporate process. "Do not be hasty in the laying on of hands", Paul tells Timothy (1 Tim. 5:22).

Here are six questions which, I hope, will clarify this for you:

1. Have you given prayerful thought to how you will invest your life for Christ?

The first question is one that **every** follower of Jesus should ask – whether considering pastoral ministry or not. Jesus' searching parable of the *talents* (or *bags of gold*) in Matthew 25:14-30 pictures a rich man going away and leaving three of his servants to invest what in today's money would be several million pounds. After a while, he comes back and asks them for an account.

The first two have taken their responsibility seriously and doubled their master's money. They understand that as servants, they must do as their master requires, and have got on with the work. As a result, they hear his wonderful commendation, "Well done, good and faithful servant", are given more responsibility, and invited to share in their master's happiness. The third servant, however, has done nothing, and reveals an attitude of resentment against his master, not trusting his good intentions. He's been lazy and fearful (the two often go together). He hasn't even bothered to put the money on deposit. He seems not really to know his master at all.

The story is so famous that the biblical word "talent" has entered the English language – though I'm not sure how many competitors in *Britain's Got Talent* know its origins! Our use of the word can make us think the parable is just about making use of the "talents" we have and being true to our gifting. In fact, in the story, the talents in the story are more accurately described as our Master's assets, which he makes us responsible for. It is part of a block of teaching Jesus gave about waiting for his second coming, and challenges everyone who calls themselves a Christian to ask how they will use their lives and all their opportunities to bring the Lord a return on what He's entrusted us with.

So then, what will you do with your millions? One day, each of us will appear before Him, and He will ask how we've invested the riches he entrusted us with to improve His assets. For not only does Christ save us, but he gives us the dignity of putting us to work for Him. Don't you want to be like one of the first two servants in the story, to whom the master said, "Well done, good and faithful servant"?

The parable is about much more than careers – about which, for Jesus' original hearers, there may not have been much choice. It's about the whole way we orientate our lives, so as to use every opportunity God has given us to maximise our Master's assets. Nor is it just about becoming a pastor: we may conclude that with the particular situation God has put us in, we may be more productive for Him in some other walk of life. This could be in the context of a regular job, through which we're able to support and serve in a local church, or in overseas mission work, or other areas. But we do **all** need, prayerfully, to be asking the question.

2. Is there evidence that you meet the New Testament requirements for the role?

We saw these in the previous chapter: the descriptions of character in the pastoral epistles, holding firm to the Apostolic message, an aptitude to teach and a willingness to suffer for Christ. Is there evidence that you have these qualities?

In terms of the call to ministry, it is particularly gifting in the area of teaching you need to think about; the other characteristics are vital but should, of course, describe every mature believer. What, then, do others think of your talks and Bible studies? Have they found them a blessing? Is there evidence of fruitfulness in your ministry to others? Is it their honest opinion that you show real promise in this area?

Obviously, as in almost everything in life, it's hard to judge potential on first attempts – for we all get better with practice. But if you keep doing it, gifting may emerge. Take opportunities, then, to give talks – at church, at the youth group, in school assemblies or Christian meetings, at summer camps – and see how you get on! Ask your pastor for opportunities. A church should seek to create such openings. At ours, we have a scheme called "Occasional Preachers", in which younger men in the congregation who are wanting to start preaching head out to churches in our region to give talks (often going with a friend who will provide moral support – and share adventures!). Men who might have the gifts for ministry give talks at our prayer meetings and in other settings.

3. Is your church behind you?

The Bible emphasises the role of others in choosing, resourcing and backing ministers of the gospel. In his famous chain of steps which are needed for people to hear the gospel, Paul asks, "And how can they hear without someone preaching to them? And how can anyone preach unless they are sent?" (Rom. 10:14b-15a). Indeed, there is more emphasis on this corporate sending than on an inward call. It was the wonderfully outreach-minded church at Antioch who sent Paul and Barnabas off on their first missionary journey (Acts 13:1-3). Titus was responsible for the appointment of leaders in Crete (Titus 1:5). A call to ministry is far from a private and personal affair: in this part of seeking God's will about whether He wants us in pastoral ministry, the role of godly friends who really know us, and above all the local church, is central. One day, you might be asking a local church to pay your salary for this role; more immediately, you may need their support for training. Do they, then, assess your potential to be worth the spend?

Get stuck in to serving in your local church and keep a conversation going with your pastor about ministry. As others observe you, they will not only be able to see your gifts, but should also be able to observe your conduct, sometimes under pressure. The opinion of others is also essential in helping see whether you meet the godly character requirements of the Bible. A healthy local church will prioritise opportunities for people's gifts to emerge in this way and be sacrificially keen to give away suitable people for ministerial training. It is part of your pastor's role in "preparing people for works of service" to do this (Eph. 4:12).

I should add that the godly counsel of others will also guard us against being self-deceived in this area and thinking of ourselves more highly than we ought. On the other hand, it may well be that others spot our suitability for pastoral ministry before we do!

4. Are you sure you understand that this will involve hard work and the pressures of leadership?

My great-grandfather was Rector of a village parish in Norfolk for over forty years. He and the family lived in a rambling rectory with a croquet lawn and tennis court; they had a full-time cook and gardener. It is worth being aware that the situation of most pastors nowadays is very different! We may serve in tough places, will be stretched, and there will be struggles and disappointments as well as great joys.

My hope is that chapter two has given you a glimpse of the nature of the job, and that chapter seven will give you some further insight. It would be worth observing what your pastor gets up to and chatting to him about what's involved.

This said, *any* leadership job has its pressures. And, interestingly, surveys of job satisfaction across professions have shown ministers scoring very highly. Rightly so: remember what Martyn Lloyd-Jones said about this office!

5. Do you have a personal desire to do this work?

When Paul writes to Timothy, "Whoever aspires to be an overseer desires a noble task" (1 Tim. 3:1), he uses two Greek verbs. The first means "to seek to accomplish a specific goal, aspire to, strive for, desire". The second means "to have a strong desire to do or secure something, desire, long for."[3] The Apostle envisages someone who really wants to do this work. And of course we'll need that desire to sustain us, to be willing to take on the demands and responsibilities we'll face. In his first letter, Peter calls the elders to be shepherds of God's flock under their care, "not because you must, but because you are willing" (1 Pet. 5:2). Surely it is this desire which is reflected in that sense of inward call referred to

---

3 BDAG.

in some ordination services, such as those in the Book of Common Prayer.

You will see that Paul's accent here is on the noble task of ministry, more than on the office of overseer. Indeed, technically the word translated overseer here is not the word for overseer, but the word for oversight.[4] The desire he's writing about is not so much to be an overseer as to do the overseer's work. Seeing this should help purify our motives, for the question is not whether we seek the status of pastor, but whether we long to be involved in doing what pastors do: feeding the Lord's sheep.

Such a desire is most likely to emerge simply out of doing such work. As we serve in our church, we may discover the joy of evangelism, the reward of teaching people in a way that grows them, the delights of seeing others mature through our personal encouragement, the satisfaction that comes through seeing the members of our Bible study or youth group built in assurance and usefulness. If we find a measure of fruitfulness attending our endeavours, we may then find that we are longing to be involved in more of this – to the extent that we want to be able to do it full-time. In many cases – my own included – people end up in paid ministry simply because they want to do more of what they're already doing, so that they can serve others more. Do you know something of that desire?

Of course we must be careful, for our desires are corrupted by sin. Check with yourself that you are not pursuing this in the search for job satisfaction, or because you like the public gaze, or a position of power, or fancy the opportunity to showcase your gifts. Or, for that matter, because you aren't succeeding in your present job. A true

---

4 See BDAG for *episkope* (oversight) versus *episkopos* (overseer). The word used here is the former. ESV's *the office of* is an interpolation.

desire for ministry will be a longing to serve the God of all grace and His people by bringing them His gospel with the gifts He's given us.

On the other hand, we shouldn't use an initial "lack of desire" as an excuse to avoid thinking about ministry, if others recognise that we might be suitable and raise the possibility with us. Neither Moses, nor Jeremiah, nor Jonah expressed any initial enthusiasm about the work God called them to! At this point we may need to be honest with ourselves and ask whether what we think of as a lack of 'desire' is actually due to a clinging to material prosperity or a fear of stepping out of a job with status. So when people who know us ask us if we've considered it, we need to be willing to enter those conversations and spread all this before God in prayer. And do expect to feel unworthy – for "who is equal to such a task?" (2 Cor. 2:16).

How does personal desire fit together with the church's role in calling and sending? Centuries ago, the Puritan preacher William Perkins answered like this:

> Would you know whether God would have you go or not? Then you must ask your conscience and ask the church. Your conscience must judge of your willingness and the church of your ability, and as you may not trust other men to judge your inclination, so you may not trust your own judgment of your worthiness or sufficiency. If your conscience truly testifies to you that you desire to serve God and his church in this calling above another; and if, upon telling this to the church and upon trial made of your gifts and learning to the church it does approve that desire, and by public calling bid you go, then surely God Himself has bid you go.[5]

---

5 I thank Ray Evans for sending me this, quoted in 'Elders and Deacons', an occasional paper by Colin Richards (Bedford Evangelical Church, 1975), p8. I have shortened the quote and put it in contemporary English.

6. Do you have a providential open door to move to this role?

In a fascinating letter, *Marks of a Call to the Ministry*, eighteenth-century pastor John Newton says, "That which finally evidences a proper call is a corresponding opening in Providence, by a gradual train of circumstances pointing out the means, the time, the place, of actually entering upon the work."[6] Newton recounts how he himself had longed to enter pastoral ministry for some years, but his path was blocked (actually, principally by resistance from the Church of England). This had frustrated him, but, looking back, he could see in God's goodness that he had not yet been ready.

It's worth asking some obvious questions. For married men, is your wife fully supportive of your training to become a pastor? This is essential – for more than many jobs, this will impact her. If she has reservations, take every necessary step to allow her to overcome them. A minister I knew felt called to ministry, while his wife did not. He took on a pastorate, but the tragic result was that they separated. Even if her reservations were wrong, the results of his going ahead were husband and wife splitting apart. It is much better – however frustrating – to wait on God's time and turn our frustrations to prayer.

It might be that there are other blockages standing in the way of an open door. Our health – or that of those we care for – might not be good enough to take on a job with these demands. We may have work or financial obligations we've entered into and which we must honour. The denominational committee might – even for wrong reasons – reject us. In each case, the right approach is to remember that we are

---

6 John Newton, *Select Letters of John Newton* (Banner of Truth, 2011), p. 54.

Christians first and potential pastors second; we must avoid folly, broken promises and ungodliness in our pathway. And we can trust ourselves into the hands of the sovereign God. This does not mean a passive fatalism – it is good to pray earnestly for the roadblocks to be removed. But knocking on the door is different from trying to knock it down!

A special word on parents. Their advice is worth hearing – they should know you well! Sometimes parents disapprove of a son's desire to become a pastor. This can be true both of non-Christians and, sadly, of some Christian parents, whose ambitions for us are less gospel-centred than they should be. This can be frustrating. But again – remembering the fifth commandment – we do well to act with respect. If we are living with them, or financially dependent on them, their opposition may make proceeding unwise or impossible. Later on, when we don't depend on them this way, we may proceed without their enthusiasm. Surely the respectful way to deal with this is to have a careful conversation, seeking their goodwill, even if it's not what they had in mind for us.

In my own case, when I mooted the idea to my parents, my father was worried. He wrote me a long letter: I'd be bored, I'd be broke and I'd be wasted! It was kind and concerned in tone. But we went out for a walk in the country and talked it through. I was able to answer him, and he gave me his blessing. In chapter six, I'll tell you whether he was proved right! But imagine my joy when, decades later, on my sixtieth birthday, I received a card from him expressing his pride and delight in my work. By now, he was reading his Bible daily and watching our church online.

* * * * *

So then: have a think about all of these questions and make them fuel for prayer. If you can answer all these questions in the affirmative, what's keeping you?

CHAPTER 5

Training

I was surprised, when I started out in ordained ministry, how much people expected me to be able to answer their questions. I shouldn't have been – I'd been to college, and now here I was as a minister in their church. It was only reasonable that they should have expected me to know what I was on about.

The question in this chapter is: what training does a pastor need? I'd like to suggest there are three components: life, specialist knowledge and on-the-job training.

The school of life

For most of us, it's useful to have had some general experience of "normal" life before heading for the pastorate. One day, we will be pastoring people whose daily experience is the workplace, and it's no bad thing to have been there ourselves, even for a short time. Here is a golden opportunity to learn what it's like to face the difficult boss, the tiresome task, the challenges of working well with customers and colleagues, and other joys of normal life. Most importantly, we will learn by experience how to live and speak for Christ in such settings – the very things we'll one day be urging others to do.

We should not underestimate what we can learn in 'the world out there'. A secular university course should develop our powers of analysis and communications – skills which are so important in the pastorate.[1] Such skills can also be developed in many lines of regular work – and it might be worthwhile, if you are privileged enough to have a choice of jobs, looking for one which will help you in these areas. Most jobs will also grow us in social skills, teamwork, reliability and personal organisation. This is also a time when you can be serving in a local church to test out your gifts and seek out whether the Lord is calling you to this ministry.

This does not need to be for a great length of time: you can learn a lot in two or three years. Nor is this the path the Lord has for everyone. Charles Spurgeon started as a pastor as a teenager. But Spurgeon was a genius, and most of us aren't. In recruiting for staff jobs at our church, I normally (though with exceptions) see experience of a 'regular' job as an advantage.

This said, an apprenticeship straight after university can be a very helpful first step: more on this below.

Specialist knowledge

What particular knowledge do we need to serve people in pastoral ministry?

First and foremost, we need to know our Bibles. Just as a doctor needs to know their anatomy, the Christian minister needs a secure grasp of Scripture. What is the letter to the

---

1 This is *not* to say that a university degree is a necessary requirement for the pastorate – but you do need qualities of mind of the kind that doing a degree might require.

Romans about? What's the storyline of Jeremiah? How do we make sense of Leviticus, and why's it there? What's the message of Habakkuk? Or Philemon?

Reading, learning and chewing over Scripture so that we know and understand it is the most important ingredient in being prepared for ministry. "I have more insight than all my teachers, for I meditate on your statutes" (Ps. 119:99), wrote the Psalmist. Simply knowing what's in the Bible is a key part of this. Scripture is our equipment: know your tools, so that you can use them.

The only way to pick this up is with consistent Bible reading. Some have found it helpful to write their own synopsis of books of the Bible as they go along. My first boss in ministry told me how, when he'd been at theological college, the students had been required to sit a weekly Bible knowledge test. It's such a good idea. In the recruitment process for staff for our church, we set just such a test.

Next to Scripture knowledge is, of course, the ability to understand it so that we can preach it responsibly. Ultimately this comes from the Spirit of God, in the process of eye-opening at conversion by which the Bible becomes a new book. But it is hugely helpful to have training in how to read the Bible in context and responsibly. Listening to reliable preaching will do a huge amount for us in this. But we'll also benefit much from teaching which gives us a thorough overview of the Bible – a biblical theology. And then we need training in the individual books. We'll learn how to work with the context, genre and flow of a passage, and how to get at the author's intention, so that we can begin to see the application for us.

An important part of preparing to be a Bible teacher is learning the biblical languages of Greek and Hebrew. This takes us behind our English translations to help us with the meanings of words, and to spot nuance and emphasis. Even a basic understanding will help us understand some points made in commentaries and will help us as we use Bible translation software.

We need a sound grasp of Christian doctrine – putting together Bible truth in a systematic way. How are we to understand the Trinity, or the resurrection of Christ, or the church, or the means of salvation? Our preaching will be more reliable when informed with such understanding, and we'll be better equipped to deal with many issues in ministry which are, at heart, theological.

Related to this is church history. We will learn the immense value of systematic theology and doctrine from another angle when we see how it has been challenged and formulated. This might save us making the same mistakes some have in the past; we'll also be encouraged as we learn of God's grace, His perseverance with His people and His reviving power.

Finally, pastoral theology will help us see how the Bible applies to the kind of issues people face in their lives. Arguably, if we have Bible knowledge, know how to read passages and have Christian doctrine under our belts, we are already part of the way there.

Do not underestimate the need for this specialist knowledge if we are to do the job well. Some might say that this makes the job look too "intellectual". Not at all: this is vital knowledge which we need to be able to help all sorts of people. When we go to a doctor, we expect them to know their stuff: how much more with the ministry of the Word of God!

Training courses

So far so good – but at this point we face a range of different ways to acquire this knowledge. There are university degree courses, theological colleges, and various local and online courses. Which is best?

The key is surely to focus not on the *means* of training, but on the *outcomes*. What we need, one way or another, is to acquire the appropriate level of knowledge in the areas set out above; how to get there matters less. Perhaps the ultimate proof of this is in the ministries of Charles Spurgeon and Martyn Lloyd-Jones, neither of whom had a formal qualification, but who were self-taught. It matters less how we acquire the expertise we need than that we have it. And each of us has different circumstances, which will control what kind of training is practical for us.[2]

This said, very few of us indeed have the skill to acquire all our knowledge via self-teaching – at least in a way that is balanced and reliable. This is why courses are so important.

A standard and very useful approach is residential theological training. Most of us find learning from a tutor in the room easiest, and it is also great to have fellow students as conversation partners (and friends in the years of ministry ahead). Often the training is to diploma or degree level – normal thresholds for the depth of learning needed for a pastor. The downside is that these are expensive – but I don't recall meeting anyone who regretted going to a

---

2 Of course, we need to be trained to an acceptable standard. It is a matter of regret that in the UK there exists no recognised common training standard for pastoral ministry, as there does for doctors or accountants, or even learning to drive! I pray that one day we'll have a mechanism for assessing this; perhaps a common Bible knowledge test shared by churches would be a start. It could be open to people from all sorts of different training routes.

good theological college. (Some of those who have been to ones with a lack of clearly evangelical and biblical ethos do have regrets.)

Increasingly and rightly, theological colleges around the world are also widening access by making some training available online. This is less disruptive and can usefully be combined with a part-time pastoral job in a church. Their online nature greatly increases the range of institutions we could enrol in, and it may be that we can do this with others at our church or some other local group.

University degree courses in Christian theology can have value – in studying the biblical languages and giving a head start in Bible books and doctrine, for instance. However, they are not intended as vocational training for ministry. Some specialise in a few topics, rather than covering a balanced range. Many degree courses are not taught from the presupposition that Scripture is the Word of God. We'd be wise not to regard such courses as a full preparation for ministry.

Bible handling courses – such as those run in the UK by Cornhill, and at a more basic level by Gospel Partnerships – are of enormous value in learning how to read the Bible and giving us a secure biblical theology. Indeed, they have more of this focus than many theological colleges. They tend not to focus so much on doctrine or history; they may offer some basic language study. Many pastors have found attending one of these courses a hugely helpful prelude to going to college.

All this said, lifelong learning will be the pastor's attitude: constantly reading and seeking to grow in understanding. College is just the start; part of its value will be getting us into the habit of being learners. After all, that's what a disciple is.

On the job training

The Lord Jesus took His disciples with Him in much of His ministry, and the Apostle Paul had a gang of people working with him – see the end of the letter to the Colossians for some names. Were these trainees? Perhaps not in an official sense, but equally, how could you spend time with Paul and not be learning from the experience? He had a great burden for the next generation (2 Tim. 2:2), and it's hard not to imagine that he consciously took men with him to learn from him. There is enormous value in learning by doing, with supervision. This is no different from many jobs – doctors, lawyers and teachers are trained this way.

Church internships/apprenticeships are a wonderful way to dip your toe into pastoral ministry. Normally these last for a year or two and are combined with attendance at a local training course. In some churches, these are encouraged for those in their early twenties, before perhaps doing a secular job for a few years and then entering ministry (or, in some cases, going on to a church staff post). Other churches prefer to recruit those who have already had some workplace experience, and, in their case, college would be the likely next step. There are arguments for each.

Some men have found working as a pastor's study assistant or personal assistant to be helpful in understanding the nature of the role. These could be done as an intern or perhaps combined with a church staff job.

Some churches have staff teams with specialist positions such as students', youth or children's worker, or evangelist. These are substantial jobs in themselves but can also be useful stepping stones to a wider pastoral role. Often these jobs fit between doing a local training course and going to college.

Finally, there are assistant minister positions in many churches – in Anglican churches, curacies. I found my curacy – under two different training ministers – to be a wonderful preparation for taking on the role of senior pastor. I made plenty of mistakes but didn't have to pick up all the pieces!

* * * * *

We have sketched out the value of the *noble task*, the qualifications needed, the call to the ministry and pathways of training. But some questions remain.

CHAPTER 6

Questions

I mentioned a while back my father's kind concerns when I mooted with him the possibility of leaving my job to train for pastoral ministry: I'd be bored, I'd be broke, and so on. You may have similar concerns for yourself! This chapter attempts honest answers to some of the questions which arise.

Will I be broke?

In the UK, pastoral ministry is modestly remunerated. At the time of writing, a Church of England minister gets about ten percent less than the national median salary, but is also supplied a house/workplace rent-free. Some other denominations and free churches pay more than this, some less. In general, pastors in the UK are paid less than their American or Australian counterparts, though more than those in some other parts of the world.

It's also the case that most men with the necessary gifts for this work could earn much more in another line of work, so there is an element of sacrifice in doing this full-time. Residential theological training adds a further pressure:

I recall how my annual grant for this was equivalent to twelve weeks' worth of my previous salary, and we had to make it last all year!

Here is a matter which UK churches ought to address: the New Testament requires that ministers are properly paid (1 Tim. 5:17-18), and churches need to heed this very practical instruction as best as they are able, valuing their ministers by putting their money where their mouths are.

This said, my own experience is that although we have had to live modestly, and at times things have been tight, God has provided. Colleagues in ministry over the decades would similarly testify to the Lord's provision, sometimes via a job their wife has been able to do, sometimes with a source of income from some part-time work, sometimes through unexpected gifts or bursaries. I – and others – could point to times when the Lord has wonderfully provided, just at the right time. We must, at the end of the day, not let money worries or a lower standard of living be a complete block to us, as it was to the rich young ruler who came to see Jesus. And we need to remember our Lord Jesus' undertaking to us – we have it in writing – "Truly I tell you … no one who has left home or brothers or sisters or mother or father or children or fields for me and the gospel will fail to receive a hundred times as much in this present age: homes, brothers, sisters, mothers, children and fields – along with persecutions – and in the age to come, eternal life" (Mark 10:29-30). Try it and see!

Might I burn out?
There is no doubt that the job has its pressures. We are engaged in a spiritual battle: the devil wishes to attack the church, and one way he can do that is by focussing on

leaders. The job also carries with it limitless opportunities to do more – visit more people, start new initiatives, and so on – and the pastor is perhaps best placed in the church to see the needs. Add to this the huge increase in requirements for due administrative process in the governance of charities, and you have the potential for long hours, some of them quite difficult. Then there are disappointments as well as joys: as the Apostle Paul wrote, "Who is weak and I do not feel weak? Who is led into sin, and I do not inwardly burn?" (2 Cor. 11:29). Some ministers have been exhausted by this, and their mental health has suffered.

But in the light of this, God is bringing churches today a greater awareness of these pressures. Christopher Ash has addressed this in two excellent books: *Zeal Without Burnout* helps Christian workers be wise about productive self-care; *The Book Your Pastor Wishes You Would Read* is aimed at elders or church councils to help them to support their pastors (because, by so doing, they will retain them and get the best results). [1] There are some other useful reads – at this point I should mention Kent Hughes' fine work *Liberating Ministry from the Success Syndrome*,[2] because sometimes burnout is caused by our own attitudes and wrong expectations.

As a result, some congregations are now much clearer about the need to ensure pastoral staff have proper days off, holidays and sabbatical leave. Churches are also waking up to the need to provide administrative support, so that their

---

1 Christopher Ash, *Zeal without Burnout: Seven keys to a lifelong ministry of sustainable sacrifice* (The Good Book Company, 2016); Christopher Ash, *The Book Your Pastor Wishes You Would Read (but is too embarrassed to ask)* (The Good Book Company, 2019).

2 R. Kent Hughes and Barbara Hughes, *Liberating Ministry from the Success Syndrome* (Tyndale, 1987).

preachers are not gagged by red tape. There is some way to go, but it is culturally much easier to talk about these kinds of things than it used to be.

It would not be sensible to enter pastoral ministry – certainly a senior pastor's position – if your health means you cannot do a proper days' work; you will also need a constitution that has some resilience in the face of pressure. The same would be true of any leadership job. It is worth noting, however, that some mental health struggles need not be a showstopper: Charles Spurgeon struggled with depression, an experience he writes about movingly as his "fainting fits" in his *Lectures to my Students*; and yet, consider how God used him!

What will the impact be on my family life?

Most British pastors work from home – their manse, vicarage, or rectory. This is unlike their American counterparts, who tend to work from an office at church. You will live in a house with many visitors, sometimes in the evenings. Sunday lunches will be times when people meet your kids – and your kids meet all sorts of interesting people! Dad will sometimes be out in the evening, and occasionally preoccupied, even when he's there. Sometimes children may struggle with not being able to use the lounge when the elders are round, or even living in a house which is not as well maintained or furnished as those of their friends at school.

This said, the pastor's home is one of the glories of the Reformation – remember, before that, ministers were unmarried. There is something beautiful about those we pastor being able to share our lives a bit – and for our children to share in the life of the church family. Ours grew up with many friendships with honorary aunts, uncles and grannies, and a real knowledge of people and how they tick. Indeed, there are few better ways for our children to become 'people people'. My wife Rachel grew up in a Rectory: they didn't have much money, but were rich in friendships, and she wouldn't swap that upbringing for the world. It's interesting how many kids who've grown up in ministry homes have gone on to be high achievers.

Will I get bored?

No. True, there are some humdrum parts of any job: routine admin and denominational meetings can be tedious. But overall, pastoral ministry really is an adventure. Real highs and real lows – yes; but seldom boredom!

What about theologically mixed denominations?

My own denomination, the Church of England, has for centuries been theologically mixed: not in its foundations, which are biblical, but in its ministers and leaders. More recently, however, a totally unbiblical revisionism is getting close to overturning even the foundations. Other older denominations have the same issues – some of them capitulating. Is it possible to serve in these with integrity?

This is a bigger subject than we can address properly here, and the landscape is changing rapidly. I can only offer some broad principles to help us do this.

First and foremost, we will take the Bible's many warnings about false teachers very seriously. Just as it is a message – the gospel – which changes lives, false messaging does great harm. We will never want to be in a situation where we give false teachers either credibility or access to our congregations. We will also be aware of our own weakness in this respect, and guard against the system drawing us into teaching falsehood ourselves.

For this reason, we will not be able with integrity to sign declarations that we can live with teaching which, at the level of sin and salvation, clearly contradicts the Bible. We will not be able to welcome such teachers to the churches we serve, nor give them our congregation's money. We must never do these things. We will only be able to serve in a denomination which tolerates false teaching if there is a clear way we can signal that we don't support that. We will need courage to teach against the falsehood, which can be a deep infection.

This said, we need to recognise that "guilt by association" is more of a cultural value (huge in an age of cancelling) than a biblical one. The Bible speaks more of the *dangers* of association. Just because there is false teaching in areas in a denomination does not necessarily mean that we must leave. The faithful in Sardis are not encouraged to do so (Rev. 3:1-6). The key is being able, within the set-up, to maintain enough distance for people to be clear we don't hold to this, never supporting it, and refusing to perjure ourselves with declarations or statements of faith or practice to which we cannot. with integrity, subscribe.

Far from false teaching being a reason to hold back from ministry, never more are faithful pastors needed than in such a context. Paul urges Timothy to "stay there in Ephesus" (1 Tim. 1:3) so that he can look after the church. The Apostle himself, writing to the Corinthians at an earlier date, says "I will stay on at Ephesus until Pentecost, because a great door for effective work has opened to me, and there are many who oppose me" (1 Cor. 16:8-9). He stays to counteract the effect of opponents of the gospel.

Perhaps most strikingly, Paul writes to Titus in the context of the spread of false teaching in Crete: "The reason I left you in Crete was that you might put in order what was left unfinished and appoint elders in every town, as I directed you … For there are many rebellious people, full of meaningless talk and deception, especially those of the circumcision group. They must be silenced …" (Titus 1:5, 10-11). As John Stott memorably puts it: "In other words, when false teachers increased, Paul's strategy was to multiply the number of true teachers."[3] Could you, supported by faithful colleagues, be part of that?

Of course, it may become necessary for many of us to break old denominational ties, along with our congregations, because we have been required to subscribe to what in conscience we cannot. But read Robin Sydserff's account (see page 83) and you will see how when he and his congregation in Scotland had to do just that, the Lord was still there for them.

Local situations also differ, and our consciences may settle in different places. It is a matter of great thankfulness that in the UK we have several denominations which are seeking to hold to Apostolic truth, and the Fellowship of Independent Evangelical Churches provides excellent support for many independent, biblically faithful churches, with great opportunities for pastors, as do various Presbyterian networks. It is also a matter of real thanksgiving that great friendships exist between gospel ministers across these denominational divides. Those of us in the Church of England are also thankful for the support of many biblically faithful friends in the Anglican set-up both in the UK and worldwide.

---

3 John Stott, quoted in Gavin Reid (ed), *Hope for the Church of England?* (Kingsway, 1986), p. 30.

How long should I wait?
There's a balance to be struck. Don't rush – there's a lot to think about. But on the other hand, our life circumstances tend to get more complicated as time goes by, and a move to training and ministry can become harder. Moreover, since it takes time to grow into the job, an earlier start means more experience on the job and sometimes more usefulness as a result.

Isn't this whole thing too much of a risk?
It *will* be a risk for you to leave the security of your present job to train for pastoral ministry. You may forfeit a degree of earthly security and status. You are stepping into something with many unknowns: where you'll end up working, how it will pan out in practice, what will happen to your denomination, and much more. You are indeed taking a risk!

But why not? Many worthwhile things in life are worth taking risks for – and surely, most of all, the gospel! In a memorable talk at London's Evangelical Ministry Assembly in 2006, *Taking risks for the glory of God*, John Piper pointed out just some examples of risk-taking in the Bible. David's commander, Joab, recognised that the outcome was uncertain when he took on the Ammonites in battle (2 Sam. 10:11-12). Esther took a huge risk when she went in to see the king (Esther 4:16). Daniel's friends didn't know the outcome when they defied Nebuchadnezzar's edict (Dan. 3:16-18). Paul was the biggest risk-taker in the New Testament – going to Jerusalem when he knew he faced danger (Acts 21:13-14).

To this we might add the Council of Jerusalem's commendation of Paul and Barnabas: they were men "who have risked their lives for the name of our Lord Jesus Christ" (Acts 15:26). So had Priscilla and Aquila (Rom. 16:4), and

Epaphroditus (Phil. 2:30). So do many pastors worldwide. Not many of us will be called to do that!

Besides, while it's possible to be rash, there is also risk in being risk-averse: a risk of mediocrity, underuse, second best. Sometimes our risk-aversion is in fact a cloak for laziness: as the proverb says, "A sluggard says, 'There's a lion in the road'" (Prov. 26:13). Don't reach the end of your earthly life having failed to maximise the gifts and opportunities God has given you, just by playing safe.

Above all, we need to believe and hold on to the promise of the Lord Jesus, given in the context of mission: "And surely I am with you always, to the end of the age" (Matt. 28:20). It is as we step out in His mission that we'll come to experience that, first hand. And what an experience that is.

You'll never see the view from the top of the Matterhorn if you don't climb it.

What if it's just not for me?
It may be that, after reading this and talking to friends you trust, and praying about these things, you conclude that pastoral ministry is just not for you. If so, fair play! The Lord knows each of us better than anyone, and our unique situations. He understands. I hope that reading the book will give you a clearer idea of what is involved, so you can pray for, and support, your pastor in his work and join him in it, as your gifts allow.

But if it is?
If you think this could be you, it is essential that you talk to your own pastor – seek his wisdom and that of the leadership of your church, as well as friends who know you and you can trust to be honest. May the Lord give you the desire of your heart!

CHAPTER 7

True Stories

What's it actually like being a pastor? What are the pressures and rewards? I asked five pastors from different settings, none of whom has fewer than twenty years' experience in the role, to tell their stories. Every situation is different, but these men can tell you something of what it's been like for them.

Ray Evans

Ray is Church Leadership Consultant for the Fellowship of Independent Evangelical Churches (FIEC). He is married to Jenny and was for four decades lead pastor at Grace Community Church, Bedford. During his time the church grew greatly in number, and there were several church plants. He started working life as an academic geographer. He supports Arsenal FC.

Jenny, my wife, and I have been blessed with four wonderful children: two boys and two girls. Without taking anything away from the privilege of having sons, one of the greatest joys of my life was walking my two daughters down the aisle to meet their husbands-to-be.

As a pastor, it was an unusual experience: first, I was (for me) very late; second, everyone was looking at me (well her, really), and then they were all smiling! But the most wonderful thing was to see him turn and look at her with such tenderness, joy and delight.

The apostle Paul uses this imagery to describe his task as a pastor (2 Cor. 11:2). You will walk with her, the church, to present her to Him, the ultimate Bridegroom. No one else has quite that privilege!

Now, as the context bears out, that mission can be fraught. Any dad will tell you of challenges in bringing his daughters to that day. One of our girls, seen dancing around after a service when she was four years old, elicited this response from an older Christian believer, "Ray, you'd better pray for an early conversion!" Well mercifully, there was. For both daughters the path to that wonderful day wasn't smooth; the waiting, though borne graciously, wasn't easy.

So it is with Christian ministry – there are challenges, but they are more than made up for by the ultimate joy of being there, watching, enjoying, exulting, when "she" meets "Him", her (and your) Saviour and Lord.

So what are some of the challenges? They are indeed serious, but they are not "front and centre". But there were some big areas I had to work at, with God's help.

For me, first, there was anxiety about "the call" and fitness to serve. But I found William Perkins' words (see above, p. 47) very helpful. I was willing to serve, and God's people assessed my fitness, and then set me apart. Of course, there then was training as Alasdair so helpfully described, but there are lots of other lessons. Here are some:

Humbling

My first elders' meeting included this, "Never think that the church has got so bad that it can't get worse under your leadership, Ray". Phew – and ouch! This was followed by, "Don't say in a year's time that I didn't tell you that it can be very difficult". That was right! Sinners, even forgiven ones, can be the cause of great concern in ministry.

Just three months later, this was followed by a commitment to church planting where our senior pastor was going to leave me to look after the main congregation on my own. I was 27, and six months into ministry. Talk about thrown in at the deep end. But it meant from early days that I was taught not to be self-sufficient.

Gifting

I followed an extremely gifted preacher (Dr. Lloyd-Jones especially prayed for him). He moved two miles down the road to plant a church. I had to work hard at my preaching if I wasn't to see the whole congregation migrate. Slowly, the gifting strengthened. Then I had to learn to listen better – people's lives are more complex than I realised. Simplistic pastoral solutions often didn't help. I was a slow learner, but gradually my pastoral care deepened and matured.

And then, in my late thirties and early forties, I had to start learning what church leadership was all about. I'm still a work in progress in all of these areas, but grateful for God, and for people's patience with me.

Teamwork

I'm so grateful for "being on a team that puts people in heaven", to paraphrase a famous saying (the NASA janitor who said, "I'm part of a team that put a man on the moon.")

It's been a joy to serve with colleagues in very small "golf buddy" type teams,[1] and then also to lead a growing team of both fellow elders and numerous staff. Being a good team player and learning what it takes to be a good team leader are key ministry skills.

Growing

A Narrative of Surprising Conversions is one of Jonathan Edwards' famous works, and the biographies of Martyn Lloyd-Jones tell of similar things. I found the stories a bit intimidating, perhaps even crushing. I wondered if anyone would get saved under my ministry!

Yet, here I am, forty years in ministry later, and I look back and can tell of God working in the most amazing, wonderful ways. I'd love to tell you of some of the stories, but space precludes that (another day for another book?). But if you stick at gospel work, I'm sure you will have some stories of "triumphs of grace" too. It is an indescribable joy.

I have also witnessed God at work growing His church where I served all my ministry life. From twelve people in 1972, when we came to a medium-sized church in 1977, to church planting several times, to growing through "awkward sized" in the "noughties" to a (small) large church of over 500 people from 2010 onwards. As one friend said, "If God can do it with Ray in Bedford, he might just do it with me here".[2] How lovely is that? I wouldn't have wanted to miss it for anything else. Several of my fellow PhD friends in time became professors of geography, and another a multimillionaire – good things – but the joy of seeing God's

---

1 Larry Osborne, *Sticky Church* (Zondervan, 1978).

2 Phil Moon, quoted in Ray Evans, *Ready, Steady, Grow: Equipping Today's Gospel Churches* (IVP, 2014).

family grow and the prospect of being there with them on the last day, means I wouldn't replace my life calling for any other.

The overarching story is of the most amazing grace of God, both in my life saving "a wretch like me", and then through me and those I've served with, in the lives of others too. May you have that joy however you serve, but especially if you serve in pastoral ministry as He leads, equips, and encourages you.

David Heath-Whyte

David is Team Rector of Morden, in South London. He is married to Clare and has been in paid local church ministry since 1998. He served churches in Chesham and Frogmore before his present post. Before ordination, David was a pilot, and that's where the story starts...

I was singing "I Stand Amazed at the Presence" at our monthly care home service. As I looked around, I was suddenly struck by the contrast between this, my "workplace", and that of my friends and former colleagues, flying their technologically advanced Dreamliners and A350s around the world. But I was glad to be there, and just moments later I read from John 4 and was talking simply about the new life that Jesus alone can give us. What an invitation: "Whoever drinks the water [Jesus gives them] will never thirst …".

At university I had decided that I wanted to work full-time in Christian ministry of some sort, involving planes, if possible, because I loved flying. British Airways were recruiting: if I could get a pilot cadetship with them, I could go on to fly for Mission Aviation Fellowship. At the same time, though, a minister at church was reading the Bible with me and recommended the "London Week" – a week of vicar-shadowing and Bible teaching. It was fantastic, and I was nearly persuaded that I should be proclaiming the Gospel as a church minister. But in the next couple of weeks, I was offered a place with British Airways.

For five years after graduating, I trained and then flew with British Airways, flying Boeing 737s and the Lockheed Tristar. During this time, I met and married Clare, and we lived in Oxford and got stuck into St Ebbe's church.

In the end, the call of frontline Gospel ministry proved more compelling. I felt that the abilities God had blessed me with fitted the role of pastor-teacher-evangelist better, and Clare and I would better be able to take part in ministry together. So, when my sponsorship bond was over, I left BA to train at Wycliffe Hall in Oxford.

My first ordained post was in Chesham (a town northwest of London) where I was a trainee assistant minister. I saw there how slow and diverse normal ministry is, compared with student work. Big surprises (to me, not God) were Julia, a single mum in her late teens, who wanted to follow Jesus after watching the *Jesus Film* on video. Then Archie and Annabel, in their 70s, from over the road, who became Christians. "Because of Jesus, I'm not afraid of dying any more" was Archie's testimony – and I had expected only younger people to become Christians! Seeing normal people, sometimes with messy lives, coming to faith in Jesus, and sticking with Him, was brilliant. It was in ones and twos, but God was at work.

After three and a half years we moved to Frogmore, a small town also north of London, where I became vicar. I was fairly young to be a vicar (34) and didn't always do the wisest things – I certainly thought my way was the best way and had to learn the art of consultation! There was a churchyard there where locals buried their dead: this had some complexities but brought lots of opportunities to speak to local people of our risen Saviour, who alone brings hope beyond the grave. In the work there, I was deeply blessed by the gift of two loyal preaching colleagues.

Paul encourages Timothy to be like a hard-working farmer, and I think my experience of parish ministry has been like that: lots of repeating tasks, week by week, that don't immediately seem to be doing much, but that add up to people coming to know Jesus, or keeping going with Jesus, or growing in Jesus. Sometimes it seems like a slog – finding time to do sermon preparation amongst the other meetings and admin tasks going on – and then occasionally you hear how something at church has helped someone with their faith in Jesus, and you remember God is at work.

Together with the church family in Frogmore we got on with lots of straightforward outreach to the community: a toddler group, kids club, old people's tea, occasional adventures with visiting door-to-door, engagement with community events. We eventually had coordinated home groups (that was a bit of a struggle), and we tried an afternoon service. It was great to see the impact of preaching that was biblical, expository and with a constant Jesus and gospel heart. I shouldn't have been surprised when Bill, who had been to various churches over the years, found a new joy in hearing God speaking through His word. Mark, who was a builder, became a Christian and then used his skills in helping the church in every building related way possible, while trying to encourage his wife and children to see what a great treasure Jesus is.

There was so much in this first job that I had not been prepared for by ordination training or the curacy. That did lead to some very stressful times – there were Sundays I didn't want to go to church, and a couple of times I found myself curled up under my study desk praying it would all go away. King David's words in Psalm 18:29b have come to be a favourite quotation of mine: "with [the help of] my God I can scale a wall". David was right – and God has always been faithful. Many "walls" have been scaled – God is good.

After twelve years in Frogmore, we felt God was calling us to move on, and to use the experience we had gained in a new setting. So now we are in Morden, a district in south London. We have the joy of being part of a like-minded clergy team: a mini Gospel-partnership across four churches.

We're loving being here: the congregations here are very diverse, a glimpse of the multi-coloured nature of heaven. Ministry continues to be a mix of the regular tasks, exciting extras, and some necessary admin. People are still coming to Christ – sometimes in extraordinary ways. Take Jason Armstrong, who was a scary arrival at my front door, but who said "Yes" to Jesus straight away, and has been transformed by God over the last few years.[3] Then Lyon (names changed from here), a single mum who felt welcomed and at home, had a full-immersion baptism. Ed, a homeless veteran who came to Christ as we helped him find accommodation. Rachel, who got baptised with a sprinkle, whose testimony surprised me again with how God uses the everyday Jesus-and-Bible-centred ministry we are part of.

---

3   You can read Jason's story in *Last on God's List: A Violent Life Transformed*, by Jason Armstrong and Clare Heath-Whyte (TenofThose, 2023).

Jesus continues to be the greatest treasure, and although I wouldn't mind a go in a Dreamliner, to have the part I do in making Him known, that "living water, welling up to eternal life" – with all his help – continues to be a joy and a privilege.

Andrew Raynes

Andrew has been Vicar of Christ Church Blackburn, Lancashire, since 1999. He is married to Chantal. His story starts thousands of miles away...

I met my wife Chantal in Pakistan where we were both working with Operation Mobilisation. As we began married life, we had a shared desire to give our lives to Christian ministry. But we didn't have a clear idea of what that might look like in the longer term.

I served as a UCCF staff worker for five years. Towards the end of this period, we began to investigate the possibility of going back to Pakistan for a longer term. However, when our second child, Alex, was born with a serious heart defect, we saw this as a clear indication that we needed to reconsider and to look at ways we could serve closer to home where Alex's medical needs could be met. As we thought and prayed and took advice from our church leaders, I felt increasingly drawn towards ordained ministry.

After training (first on the Cornhill Training Course and then at theological college) I spent four years as an assistant minister (curate) in Crowborough, a commuter town in East Sussex. It was after that that we moved up to Blackburn.

This felt like a big move at the time. I think that one of the big motivations in coming here was to be in an area where (at that time at least) it felt that the gospel was less well-known than in other parts of the country. I remember hearing Michael Green recount a conversation he had with a senior churchman, who drily remarked, "You evangelicals do love the south coast, don't you?" I'm not sure that's entirely fair, but if it ever was, there is now a growing number of evangelical ministers serving in the north-west of England.

Around two-thirds of our parish population are Muslims from an Indian or Pakistani background. Over the years that I've been here, we have seen a growing number of internationals moving into the parish, many of whom have made Blackburn their home. We have a church school, where almost all the pupils are from Muslim homes.

I inherited a congregation that was entirely white Anglo-Saxon in its makeup. The church family is now a glorious mix of nationalities and much more reflective of the area we serve. We are steadily learning to be an intercultural church, united around the gospel but culturally very flexible on how we do things, including the food we eat and the songs we sing.

We are not a large church with a big budget, but in the Lord's goodness, we have been able to take on a variety of people to serve in paid ministry. A lot of youth and children's ministry, for example, is led by volunteers.

My biggest battle is to keep going in the ministry of the Word "in season and out of season" (2 Tim. 4:2), keeping the prayerful proclamation of the gospel at the core of what I'm about. I regularly need to remind myself of God's sovereignty in ministry: remembering that the Lord Jesus is the Chief Shepherd, that ministry will involve disappointments as well as joy.

In periods when church life seems hard, when my own heart is not thrilled with Jesus, I go back to passages such as 2 Corinthians 4 or the parable of the Sower in Mark 4 to reset my own expectations of what genuine gospel ministry looks like.

I found Kent and Barbara Hughes' book, *Liberating Ministry from the Success Syndrome*, a great challenge to the prideful me that wants to be building my own empire or leading a "successful" church. I have learned to be able to say (on my best days): "I may be in what some would consider a bit of a backwater, but I have the great privilege of being pastor of Christ's flock in this place – and I want to be faithful and to live with my eyes on Him and not on my reputation among my peers".[4]

The most draining periods of ministry have come when there has been relational strain. Thankfully these have been rare, but my first few years in Blackburn were difficult, and I encountered real hostility from people I had expected to be welcoming and supportive. In God's kindness, there were a few men who just encouraged me to keep going – and eventually things did turn round.

One of the joys of being in the same place for a while is seeing the Lord's work in people's lives over the long haul. During a "Hope Explored" course a while ago, one young man in my discussion group was someone who'd been part of our toddler group two decades ago. Most of the funerals I take these days are for people who have been part of the church family for many years.

A while back, I led the wedding service of a couple who had recently come to faith in Christ. They already had two children together but now wanted publicly to bring their relationship under the lordship of Christ: a beautiful example of God's powerful gospel at work.

---

4 Kent and Barbara Hughes, *Liberating Ministry from the Success Syndrome* (Tyndale House, 1987).

Another joy of these past few decades is to see several people who have been sent from our church now serving in ministry around the country. It's always painful to see key leaders moving on, and yet time and again the Lord has brought new people to us, and we have been the beneficiaries of the work of other churches both in the UK and beyond.

As the pastor of a smaller church, one vital source of encouragement has been through fellowship with other evangelical leaders locally. As a subgroup of our regional gospel partnership, a few of us have been able to pray together, to support one another, and to organise joint evangelistic and training events on a scale that would not have been possible for one church alone.

Pastoral ministry is indeed "a noble task": it is never dull, sometimes heartbreaking, always demanding. But it is the most important work in the world.

Orlando Saer

Orlando has been Lead Pastor of Christ Church, Southampton, since 2011. He is married to Libby. He tells us here not only how the Lord led him to pastoral ministry in the first place, but how the Lord has shaped him in the middle of it...

'Consider what I say, for the Lord will give you understanding in everything' (2 Tim. 2:7).

It was during my 'gap year' that I found myself challenged to pursue vocational ministry. I was stirred by the testimony of some missionaries I met in Bolivia who'd made it their life's work to bring the Bible and its message to an unreached tribe. I found I couldn't think of a better way of spending my years than bringing the Word of God to people who didn't have it. I continue to believe it was a conviction sent by God. I became full of ambition to be part of growing God's kingdom in some way.

But as I started out on a pathway towards ministry a few years later, it quickly became apparent that I needed a few corners knocking off me. I thought I already knew a thing or two and my default setting was to back myself. As I look back, I'd clearly missed a lot of things about humility, patience and self-awareness!

But I'd missed something else too: the tense of the verb in 2 Timothy 2:7 (see above). In case you glided over it, let me point out the obvious. It's neither a past nor a present, but a future. Yes, Paul had much guidance to offer Timothy. But grasping it would be a process, not instant. To 'consider' takes time. I suspect that's the way things have turned out for most who follow in Timothy's footsteps. It certainly has been for me. Ongoing growth in understanding has been an ongoing need – and reality –throughout my own ministry life.

Since finishing theological training – a full-fat, four-year residential experience in my case – I've held three church roles: an 'Assistant Minister' role in London suburbia, an established 'Senior Pastor' role in a small town, and a Planter-Pastor role in a city context.

The first was an opportunity to grow in my *pastoral convictions*. Fresh from college and reporting to an energetic minister who shared some of my ecclesiological convictions but not others, I had three and a half formative years. I was quickly thrown into the deep end: leading a ministry among twenty-somethings, preaching regularly, discipling individuals, trying my hand at school assemblies, weddings, mentoring ministry trainees, planning evangelistic events and much more. But all the time, I was – perhaps more than I even realised at the time – watching the show, learning the ropes and penning over the pencil of my own convictions about the priorities and rhythms of a healthy ministry. These were foundational years for developing a reliance on God's Word for God's work: I was learning what it means that 'unless the Lord builds the house, the builders labour in vain' (Ps. 127:1). They were thrilling years, and all the more enjoyable for having the buck stopping somewhere other than with me!

In many ways my second main role was more a phase of growth in *pastoral wisdom*. If you're wondering if that's meant to be code for a pretty testing experience, then you've understood me correctly. Most full-time pastors will, at some point, step into a sole or senior pastor role. And depending on the context, that transition can be an abrupt change of gear in terms of responsibility, expectations, and pressure. For me, a number of aspects of the context (and of course the limits of my own experience and wisdom) combined to create a perfect storm of testing: while the community spirit was strong and there were some really wonderful people, it was a church with a history of factionalism, powerful families and problematic leadership structures – and there were few alternative church options for unhappy members to choose.

Put those things together, and you'll likely understand why those 7½ years offered me a wonderful opportunity to get some of those corners ground off me, as well as learn to get alongside a wide variety of different people coming from different places. They were challenging years, but formative ones. The great Charles Spurgeon once said, 'It is a sweet mercy to have to go through the floods, if some filthiness may thereby be removed. The children of Israel went down to Egypt to sojourn there, but after hard servitude and cruel oppression they came up out of it with silver and gold, much enriched by their bondage.'

Which leaves my third role, leading a church from its planting. This has been – and continues to be – very much a period of growth in *pastoral leadership*. The ministry I'm involved with currently is busy, active and growing. For some, the pace would be exhilarating; for others, it would be exhausting. I think, for me, it's perhaps both in equal measure– though I wouldn't change it for anything! The 'blank sheet' of a church plant situation provides rich opportunities for shaping the culture and ministry of a church for years to come, but that opportunity is also a precious stewardship, and I've felt the responsibility of that deeply.

The rapid expansion of the work, the size of the team and the change in phases of the church's life have all meant I've had to keep growing in leadership: each year has brought fresh awareness of my own inadequacy for the task, and the need to shift gear and reconsider the shape of the ministry and my role in it. But it's been a challenge I've enjoyed and felt sustaining and equipping grace to meet.

As you can see, there have been different contexts and roles – and different learning opportunities associated with them. But so many things have been constant. Certainly, the kind of ministry Alasdair has described so clearly in this book is the ministry I've aspired to and sought to pursue throughout.

Robin Sydserff

> *Since 2024 Robin has been Director of the Proclam-*
> *ation Trust, which exists to multiply faithful Bible*

ministry, through training and resourcing of preachers. For fifteen years before that, Robin was Senior Minister of Chalmers Church in Edinburgh (previously St Catherine's Church). He is married to Sally.

After leaving University in 1992, I trained as a Chartered Accountant, followed by four years teaching accountancy and finance at university, while studying for a PhD in Business Ethics. Sally and I met and married. But pastoral ministry was always on our hearts.

So it was that the time came to apply to the Church of Scotland. Accepted as a candidate, in autumn 2000, I began three years of study at New College in Edinburgh, serving my final placement at St Catherine's from 2003–04. Unknown to us then, this was to be our first of two spells at St Catherine's. It was a wonderful time, experiencing all the privileges of ministry, with few of the responsibilities of leadership. My boss, Victor, let me preach at one of the services most weeks. We grew to love the church family.

All set to move to a church as a minister, the Lord took us by surprise, and we ended up in London at the Proclamation Trust. I had the privilege of working with Dick Lucas, David Jackman and Christopher Ash. They were wonderful years, instilling in me deep convictions that have been tested and proved in local church ministry; in particular, convictions about the Word of God. First, the transforming power of the ministry of the Word to make and grow disciples. Second, the shepherd care of the Lord Jesus for His people through the ministry of the Word, pertinent to every circumstance of life. Third, that the ministry of the Word is to be released through the life of a church, equipping everyone to speak

Jesus' Word. Multiplying Word ministry multiplies the means of transformation.

Four years later, the Lord brought us back to St Catherine's. Ever since my training placement there, they were the church family I had longed to serve. Graciously, the Lord granted the desire of my heart, and I was appointed minister in January 2009.

In the first few years, the Lord was pleased to grow the church numerically, but more importantly through a culture of training people in Word ministry. At the beginning, the staff team was small – myself, a part-time student worker and an administrator – so the focus was on equipping people who had other jobs. With busy lives, it was hard to find a time to meet, so we began a Sunday breakfast preaching group. I was exhausted by the end of a Sunday but energised by this group. Baby steps at the start, which, over the years, developed into a church-wide training culture at multiple levels.

Training vocational gospel workers was a natural progression. At the end of 2009 the church started The Bonar Trust, to develop and fund training across Scotland. In 2010, St Catherine's launched its own training programme, the Ministry Associate Programme (MAP, for short). We praise God for the 50 or so gospel workers trained over the years, and that the Bonar Trust was able to raise and invest nearly £5 million in funding people to train. Equipping many people to speak Jesus' Word and training gospel workers is a hugely rewarding investment of time and energy. In the good times, yes, but in the hard times, training was the lifeline that kept me afloat.

Every church will go through hard times. This is to be expected, because the wisdom of God is made known through the Church (local churches scattered across the world) to the rulers and authorities, the cosmic powers over this present darkness, the spiritual forces of evil (Eph. 3:10, 6:12). Satan, the Prince of this world, though a defeated enemy, will do everything in his power to destroy churches. The hardest time for us was leaving the Church of Scotland over its rejection of the Bible as the rule of faith and life. In June 2014, ninety percent of the church family left, with us, to form Chalmers Church. All we took were 300 committed people and a lectern: no money, no buildings. The symbolism was an enduring symbol of all that mattered – the people of God shepherded by the Word of God. Through the ministry of the Word, Sunday by Sunday and in small groups, the Lord Jesus shepherded us corporately as a church. These were days when the Word was wonderfully, awesomely relevant. Through His Word proclaimed Jesus kept us, guided us, changed us and liberated us from distractions and preferences.

As a church leader, you are called to bear the costs not only with others, but for others. Perfectly embodied in Jesus, exemplified by the apostles and taught to Christian ministers, as Jonathan Leeman puts it in his excellent book, *Authority*, it is the privilege of displaying and participating in Christ's redemptive cost-bearing authority.[5] There is no false piety or ascetic pleasure in this. It is hard, very hard. The cost and the scars will always be there. Yet our experience brought Jesus so close, proving the conviction that Jesus' Word was everything we need (2 Pet. 1:3). Corporately as leaders, and as a congregation, it bound us together in deep bonds of

---

5   Jonathan Leeman, *Authority: How Godly Rule Protects the Vulnerable, Strengthens Communities, and Promotes Human Flourishing* (Wheaton: Crossway, 2023).

love. It was through this experience that Sally and I were overwhelmed with the truth that these are the people God has given us to love. To be set apart as a minister or pastor in a local church is to be given by the Lord a people to love, His people entrusted to your love and care. Though I am no longer their pastor, I still love them. I will always love them. I will ever thank the Lord for His gift of them to me to love.

There are two other dimensions of love a minister experiences. First, love for the lost. You become acutely conscious and burdened by the plight of a lost humanity and yet you are afforded many opportunities to tell people the gospel. Every convert is precious and treasured in your heart. Aware of what eternity will mean, to be used of the Lord to save one soul, renders a lifetime of ministry worth it.

The second love is, in truth, the first and highest love – love for the Lord Jesus. Though fitful at times, the overall trajectory of Christian ministry is an ever-deepening devotion to Jesus. Ministry fuels the new affection that overpowers every rival affection. The challenge is guarding against anything surpassing devotion to the Lord, including devotion to the Lord's work. Yet it is engagement in the Lord's work, that with the right perspective, develops devotion to the Lord.

To be a minister is truly a noble task. It is hard, often very hard, but there is no more privileged calling. Now out of front-line ministry, my conviction is to give all my energies to encouraging, equipping and training people for ministry.

CHAPTER EIGHT

Peter's Call

To the elders among you, I appeal as a fellow elder and a witness of Christ's sufferings who also will share in the glory to be revealed: Be shepherds of God's flock that is under your care, watching over them— not because you must, but because you are willing, as God wants you to be; not pursuing dishonest gain, but eager to serve; not lording it over those entrusted to you, but being examples to the flock. And when the Chief Shepherd appears, you will receive the crown of glory that will never fade away.

—1 Peter 5:1-4

We've seen the nobility of the task of pastor in the Bible, the qualifications for the job and how you can discern whether this might be for you. We've thought about training and practical questions which arise. Real-life pastors have told their stories. But before I say, "over to you", I want to leave the last word to the Apostle Peter. Writing to scattered

Christians in the mid first century, he specifically addresses the role of pastors. We need to hear what he says.

First, *pastors are needed for God's flock*. "Be shepherds of God's flock that is under your care", he writes. He's not actually calling people to enter ministry but exhorting existing leaders to get on with looking after the flock under their care.

The picture of leaders serving people as a shepherd looks after a flock isn't one most of us have first-hand experience of. Perhaps the fact that James Rebanks' memoir *The Shepherd's Life* shot up the UK bestseller lists shows how intrigued we are by what shepherds do. [1] Suffice it to say that this is a difficult but vital job which – now, as in Peter's day – involves protecting the sheep from danger, stopping them from straying, rounding them up and bringing them to good pasture. Flocks need shepherds – they can't look after themselves. If Peter's readers were to stand firm, they needed to be shepherded!

Second, *good pastors are needed*. Peter sets out three contrasts. First, "not because you must, but because you are willing". There is no place for time-serving here: the job is inseparably bound up with a love for the Lord Jesus and His people. Second, "not pursuing dishonest gain but eager to serve". Sadly, a position of influence could be misused to extract money for personal gain: we must never go there. Rather, our attitude must be that of our Master: of serving, rather than being served (Mark 10:45). Third, "not lording it over those entrusted to you, but being examples to the flock".

Notably, Peter's response to the existence of bad pastors is not to scrap the role, but to appeal to his readers to do the

---

1 James Rebanks, *The Shepherd's Life: A Tale of the Lake District*, (Penguin, 2015).

job properly. And Peter wouldn't be calling us to impossible principles. It is actually possible, in God's strength, to be a pastor who really does serve well. I thank God for many I know who are just like that, and to whom I myself look up to as examples.

Third, *Peter needs to **exhort** the elders to do this work*. At first sight, it's curious that Peter needs to exhort these elders to "be shepherds of God's flock". After all, these men already had a senior position in their churches. Why did he have to say this at all?

The most plausible answer is surely that the world of Peter's readers involved suffering for being a Christian, and that by stepping up to pastor the flock, a man put himself especially in the line of fire. So, as Peter writes, pastoral heads are below the parapet. But for the health of the churches, they need to pop up.

In our age, with our own society's opposition to Christianity, we may be similarly tempted not to be so public a Christian as a pastor. Indeed, you may have been put off by seeing examples of faithful pastors under fire.

Peter's answer is not to pretend that no such suffering exists. Rather, he takes us back to the cross. He writes as "a fellow elder and a witness of Christ's sufferings". He was there when the Saviour was led away on trial, and the Lord's saving death has been the centrepiece of his own preaching ever since. As the Lord suffered for others, so, in a smaller way, will those who walk in the Saviour's footsteps.

If we shrink back from serving in this way just because there is a cost, we would do well to fix our eyes again on the Lord Jesus, who, in love, gave Himself for us.

Fourth, *a crown of glory lies ahead*. Peter says: "And when the Chief Shepherd appears, you will receive the crown of glory that will never fade away". Peter's letter is suffused with a sense of anticipation of the glories to come when Christ is revealed (1 Pet. 1:7, 11, 13, 4:13, 5:10). This is a certain prospect for all who belong to Him, but Peter is especially keen here for those who pastor the flock well to know that for them there is a particular reward. Even in this life, there is great reward in pastoral ministry. As Paul tells deacons, "those who have served well gain an excellent standing and great assurance in their faith in Christ Jesus" (1 Tim. 3:13). But there will be great reward when the Lord is revealed.

What this is, we can only speculate. Is it the joy of having our Master say, "Well done, good and faithful servant" (Matt. 25:21)? Or might it be the sheer joy of seeing those we've served presented mature to Christ in glory (Col. 1:28)? As someone once said of pastoral ministry, "The pay may not be great, but the prospects are out of this world!"

Finally, and most remarkably, Peter adds an astonishing extra truth: Jesus is "the Chief Shepherd." *Jesus is a pastor*! And this is not the first time in the letter Peter has said this: he's already described the Lord as "the Shepherd and Overseer of your souls". It is His present work to pastor His flock.

What higher dignity could be given to pastoral ministry than the fact that our Lord Jesus Christ is Himself a pastor?

Truly this work of ministry is *A NOBLE TASK*.

For Further Reading

One book which is especially helpful in going into the work of the pastor in more detail is Derek Prime and Alistair Begg's *On Being A Pastor* (Chicago: Moody, 2013).

As well as this, I recommend the inspiring value of reading the biographies of men like Newton, Spurgeon and Ryle. Ryle's *Eighteenth Century Christian* Leaders (republished by EP Books, Welwyn, 2018) tells the story of how God used pastors in different places to change England 280 years ago. And read, and re-read, the Pastoral Epistles.

Christian Focus Publications

Our mission statement
Staying Faithful

In dependence upon God we seek to impact the world through literature faithful to His infallible Word, the Bible. Our aim is to ensure that the Lord Jesus Christ is presented as the only hope to obtain forgiveness of sin, live a useful life and look forward to heaven with Him.

Our Books are published in four imprints:

⟨⊙⟩ CHRISTIAN FOCUS

Popular works including biographies, commentaries, basic doctrine and Christian living.

⟨⊙⟩ MENTOR

Books written at a level suitable for Bible College and seminary students, pastors, and other serious readers. The imprint includes commentaries, doctrinal studies, examination of current issues and church history.

⟨⊙⟩ CHRISTIAN HERITAGE

Books representing some of the best material from the rich heritage of the church.

⟨⊙⟩ CF4KIDS

Children's books for quality Bible teaching and for all age groups: Sunday school curriculum, puzzle and activity books; personal and family devotional titles, biographies and inspirational stories – because you are never too young to know Jesus!

Christian Focus Publications Ltd,
Geanies House, Fearn, Ross-shire,
IV20 1TW, Scotland, United Kingdom.
www.christianfocus.com